Praise for *World Class IT*

"Technology and business leaders alike must understand how to use IT to their advantage. Today, all businesses are technology companies powered by people; it is simply a question of degree. Failure to understand this and to harness technology to a company's advantage will result in one's company being a follower in an industry as opposed to a shaper of it. In *World Class IT*, Peter High distills the key principles for business and IT leaders to follow to ensure that your company is a leader rather than a laggard."
—Robert Willett, CEO, Best Buy International

"*World Class IT* taps the experience and advice of the world's greatest thinkers in corporate technology and marries it with a simple, yet powerful working framework. Peter's access to the best-of-the-best CIOs and his ability to boil their learnings down to the essentials is invaluable."
—Gregor Bailar, former chief information officer, Capital One, and former chief information officer, NASDAQ

"Peter High has made a valuable, highly practical, and rigorous contribution to principles-based IT resource management. His IT management principles are products of insightful observations in first-hand work with accomplished CIOs. Peter has observed these CIOs transforming IT management in their organizations from a narrow 'spectator support' for their senior management teams to a 'participative sport' resulting in a strategic IT asset. This is an important read for CIOs and their IT management teams."
—Richard Nolan, the Philip M. Condit Endowed Chair in Business Administration at the University of Washington, Foster School of Business, and the William Barclay Harding Professor of Business Administration at the Harvard Business School (emeritus)

"Peter High has uncovered and illuminated important principles that are relevant to any IT executive. We find that many of our most successful IT strategies are reflected in his framework, and I certainly learned from his research, as well."

—Randy Spratt, executive vice president, chief information officer, and chief technology officer, McKesson

"Following the principles and subprinciples of *World Class IT* offers invaluable insights and will improve performance no matter the company."

—Tim Harvey, former executive vice president of shared services and chief information officer, Hilton Hotels Corporation

World Class IT

World Class IT

Why Businesses Succeed When
IT Triumphs

Peter A. High

Foreword by John Boushy

JOSSEY-BASS
A Wiley Imprint
www.josseybass.com

Published by Jossey-Bass
A Wiley Imprint
989 Market Street, San Francisco, CA 94103-1741—www.josseybass.com

Jossey-Bass books and products are available through most bookstores. To contact Jossey-Bass directly call our Customer Care Department within the U.S. at 800-956-7739, outside the U.S. at 317-572-3986, or fax 317-572-4002.

Jossey-Bass also publishes its books in a variety of electronic formats. Some content that appears in print may not be available in electronic books.

Library of Congress Cataloging-in-Publication Data
High, Peter.
 World class IT: why businesses succeed when IT triumphs/Peter High; foreword by John Boushy.—1st ed.
  p. cm.—(The Jossey-Bass business & management series)
 Includes bibliographical references and index.
 ISBN 978-0-470-45018-5 (cloth)
 1. Information technology—Management. 2. Information technology—Economic aspects. 3. Management information systems. I. Title.
 HD30.2.H543 2009
 004.068—dc22

                                                            2009033970

Printed in the United States of America
FIRST EDITION

HB Printing   10 9 8 7 6 5 4 3 2 1

The Jossey-Bass
Business & Management Series

Contents

For Michelle, who is in a class by herself

Foreword

Welcome to your World Class IT journey. Regardless of your background—whether you are an IT professional or a business user of IT—you should find this book easy to read, insightful, and applicable to your industry—past, current, or future. It undoubtedly will become one of the seminal, timeless treatises on the topic of achieving World Class IT.

Some of you may be curious about what World Class IT means and how you get there—you will find satisfaction to your curiosity. Some of you may be wondering what a journey toward World Class IT requires—you will find meaningful, illustrative insights through the examples that Peter cites. Some of you may already be committed to the journey toward World Class IT and wish to "turbo-charge" your efforts—the structure provided by Peter's five principals can significantly accelerate your progress. And, some of you may already be well on your journey toward World Class IT—you will find confirmation that you are already doing many of the "right things," as well as items that undoubtedly will complement, enhance, and "fill the gaps of" your current actions.

There is value for everyone from World Class IT, for every IT department and for every business. You will likely finish the book knowing more about the "what, why, and how" of World Class IT, along with some of your own thoughts about applying your learnings to your everyday pursuit. But there is value only if you do something, like apply your learning starting yesterday!

Striving to become "world class" can seem overwhelming—there are a lot of nontrivial things to do. This challenge can seem absolutely ginormous! So when asked, "How do you eat an elephant?" meaning when the challenge seems so large, where does one begin, I respond, "One byte at a time, and invite a lot of friends." When it comes to the pursuit of World Class IT, Peter's insights, examples, and the five principals that are documented throughout this book, along with his consulting practice, are definitely "friends" that can assist an organization's achievement of World Class IT.

The five principles provide a powerful framework to conceptualize, innovate, plan, execute, and evaluate progress toward World Class IT, regardless of your current circumstances and state of execution. Harrah's is well known for developing and implementing closed-loop capabilities in the consumer-oriented marketing arena. The execution of the five principals, which includes balanced scorecards, offers an effective way to identify and track continuous improvement, which we applied to managing the business of IT with great success. One example follows.

But first, I have a confession: I was one of the people to whom Peter refers in Chapter Five who asked the question, "Why isn't alignment priority number one?" (If you want to know more, you'll have to read the chapter.) In fact, I asked Peter this question a number of times over the past seven years and did so as recently as shortly before Peter completed this work. Fortunately, Peter is patient and diplomatic, and has allowed me to learn at my own pace, which in this instance, I am sad to say, was slower than I would like. He is also "right" on this point. Here's why:

Prior to its introduction to World Class IT's five principles, Harrah's had been on its World Class IT journey for a little over four years, and we had received both internal and external recognition for making a tremendous amount of progress. Our journey began in the late 1990s because of a comment by Phil Satre, our CEO, during a review of our attempts to work with the business. His comment, "Physician heal thyself!" caused needed self-reflection within the IT department that precipitated the journey toward becoming world class. Along with this challenge of self-improvement, our journey was fueled by a strategic imperative to enhance Harrah's competitive position. Once we established this goal, we built the IT organization and processes to substantiate the marketing and operations capabilities necessary for Harrah's to improve its competitive position. A key contributing factor to our progress was the embodiment of the philosophies "what gets measured gets managed" and "doing the right things, right" from a business perspective. Our initial scorecards skewed heavily toward people, projects, and business-centric value creation. Several years of substantial improvement earned "a seat at the table" when setting overall business strategy, fine-tuning it, and suggesting modifications to it. By 2002 Harrah's business strategies were actually being strongly influenced or in several cases driven by its IT capabilities. The alignment between IT and the business was very tight and substantial.

However, our greatest strengths—partnering with the business and managing projects and portfolio effectively—had actually created an unrecognized imbalance that unknowingly threatened the very foundation of IT's ability to continuously and consistently deliver business value.

In retrospect, we did not pay nearly enough attention to the entirety of infrastructure. We were so focused on (and very good at) delivering value on behalf of the business that we prioritized business-facing initiatives *too* far ahead of infrastructure initiatives. When we implemented the World Class IT scorecards described in this book, there were lots of "blanks" or "not measured" in the infrastructure scorecard. This evaluation uncovered that we had paid shockingly little attention to disaster recovery and business continuity, which almost by definition is the exclusive realm of IT as opposed to the business. On the basis of this insight, we concluded that these areas were significantly underfocused and as a result underfunded. Moreover, our lack of focus on these areas threatened the company's ability to drive revenue in the event of an IT catastrophe.

In response to this "discovery" we presented a solid business case and received funding to correct this imbalance in a relatively short amount of time because we had a track record for delivering business value, a strong partnership with the business, and a compelling justification to "not do nothing." Thankfully, we never experienced an outage while we were unprepared to recover or continue operations. As you journey through World Class IT, there may be a similar surprising revelation awaiting you!

As you implement the principles of World Class IT, your experience will likely be different from that of Harrah's, or United Airlines, or McKesson's, or Best Buy's, or other referenced companies in Peter's work. The areas of focus may change, the challenges may change. However, the framework provided by the five principles of World Class IT offers a powerful roadmap to enhancing your current position. When and where will you begin?

As we all know, "nothing breeds success like success." An IT organization that progresses toward being world class likely not only will affect its own strategies and actions but will strongly influence the entire organization because of its success. Thus, the IT department's success can lead the organization in an exemplary fashion. Start leading by results and example!

Great accomplishments are rarely the output of just one person, or just a sophisticated set of strategies, or just the result of a compelling set of principles. Truly great results come in part from a coordinated, collaborative team effort and from the commitment of the entire team to being "world class." A corollary effect of the team's commitment is the exceptionally powerful motivation that striving to become or stay world class offers the IT professional's psyche. At Harrah's we forged a world-class series of IT and business capabilities, all in the pursuit of driving world-class business results. When we started, we were far from being World Class IT; with every month and year that went by, we made progress toward our goal. As Peter describes, the performance of one principle complements, enhances, and supports the other principles. In this instance, commitment and progress toward World Class IT strengthened principle 1, thereby developing a positive, self-perpetuating cycle throughout the IT organization.

While there are many people who worked with me to systematically drive the approaches and projects throughout IT and the business, I want to specifically acknowledge some of my colleagues: Bruce Rowe, Pat Watts, Tracy Austin, Tim Stanley, Rich Mirman, David Norton, and Gary Loveman. Last, but certainly not least, thanks to Eileen Cassini, who was inspirational, passionate, and forceful about winning the wallets, the minds, and, most important, the hearts of IT professionals as a requisite condition to building World Class IT. Along with key leaders in the business and the entire collection of IT professionals, this team has imprinted an indelible mark on IT, not only at Harrah's but for many IT professionals who aspire to contribute real business value through the pursuit of World Class IT.

A final thought: occasionally I wonder how much progress we would have made had we met Peter and embraced the five principles earlier. Much of our early progress was due to continuous improvements through experience. Fortunately, our experience was pretty good due to frequent herculean efforts on the part of our IT professionals. While we almost always focused on the right things, sometimes we did not focus on all the right things we should have. This book offers a prescriptive, holistic, pragmatic, "battle tested," and aspirational roadmap to guide and evaluate progress toward World Class IT. You can pioneer (in your company) without being a pioneer!

So get comfortable to begin the rewarding, but neverending journey of World Class IT.

John Boushy
Las Vegas, Nevada
July 2009

The Author

Peter A. High is the founder and president of Metis Strategy, LLC, a business and information technology strategy consultancy founded in 2001. His experience lies in corporate strategy, business-unit strategy, information technology strategy, and all of the areas covered by the principles and subprinciples of World Class IT.

Peter developed the World Class IT Methodology within months of founding the firm, and he and his colleagues have implemented it at many companies in a wide range of industries, including financial services, insurance, business process outsourcing, retail, pharmaceuticals, health care, travel and transportation, and media. Peter has advised business and information technology executives in the Americas, Europe, Asia, and Africa.

Peter has lectured at a number of leading business schools, including Georgetown University's McDonough School of Business and the University of Washington (Seattle) Foster School of Business. He also hosts a widely heard podcast called "Metis Strategy's Forum on World Class IT." Peter has been an ongoing contributor to *Information Week* and *CIO Digest*.

Peter graduated from the University of Pennsylvania with degrees in economics and history. He lives in Chevy Chase, Maryland, with his wife and their two sons. He can be reached at peter.high@metisstrategy.com.

Acknowledgments

In January 2002, I had the great fortune of working with John Boushy, senior vice president and chief information officer of Harrah's Entertainment, and Tim Stanley, who would succeed John soon thereafter. Harrah's had (and still has) one of the great IT departments in the United States. The IT department was highly regarded by the entire company, and associates in the business even thought about ways to migrate over to IT. Even today, this is not the typical migratory path of employees at most companies.

The company had remarkably low attrition. Even during the dot-com boom, which had come to an end less than a year before, the IT department had lost relatively few employees, which was also quite unusual. As a result, the talented IT department had a long collective memory. What John and Tim came to realize, however, was that the success of the department relied on its people's memories too much, and should some of those people elect to leave, there might not be adequate processes in place to ensure that high performance could be sustained. That is when they asked us to help them define a methodology to sort this out. Thus, the principles in this book began to take shape. World Class IT was born. Having now worked with a great number of companies since that initial World Class IT engagement, I know that Harrah's Entertainment's starting point on the path to World Class IT performance was high because they had already accomplished so much under the stewardship of such strong leaders, and John and Tim continue to be model CIOs in my mind. I have been proud to continue to collaborate with Harrah's IT.

In November of 2008, I launched a podcast called "Metis Strategy's Forum on World Class IT." I have had the pleasure of speaking with many clients and other friends and contacts about the principles discussed in this book. This has added many great stories from IT leaders in business and academia, some of which I have drawn into this project.

Along the way, I have had the honor of working with many great colleagues whose fingerprints are all over the methodology. Melanie Drouet worked with me as the World Class IT Methodology began to take shape and as the principles were defined with Harrah's. Laurent Guinand played a critical role in refining many of the subprinciples that will be described throughout this book. In addition, Chris Davis has provided invaluable research for this book. Christian Dully has worked hard on research related to our World Class IT work, but he has also had a heavy hand in our podcast, and I am grateful for his efforts. I also would like to thank Alex Kraus, who has been my primary collaborator over the past five years. He has offered support and guidance for which I am grateful.

I would also like to thank the wonderful people at Jossey-Bass who made this such a smooth and enjoyable process. I would like especially to thank Rob Brandt, Dani Scoville, and, most of all, Kathe Sweeney. They have helped keep this project on track in addition to providing great advice on how to organize my thoughts.

Last, I would like to thank my wife, Michelle, and our sons, Alex and David, who spent less time with me than all of us would have liked during the course of this project. I am lucky to have them, and their love and support has meant the world to me.

Introduction

Prior to the 1970s, computer and electronics-based technology was hardly a pervasive part of our everyday lives. Automobiles were not yet computerized, fax machines were just taking off, and, significantly, the personal computer had yet to be popularized. Individuals who dreamed of a career in information technology departments were likely those who happened to come into contact with technology. Microsoft founders Bill Gates and Paul Allen famously attended the Lakeside School in Seattle together that had a time-shared PDP-10 computer, which allowed them to learn computer programming and, equally important, to dream big dreams that would have an impact on us all.

Today technology is everywhere. Some of us are awakened by clocks that are MP3 players, have coffee makers that operate on electronic timers, navigate the routes we drive each day with global positioning systems (GPSs), check in to flights and select our seats before we arrive at the airport, and operate Blackberries to send and receive email messages with colleagues wherever in the world we may be.

Today we are all technologists, insofar as we interact with technology every day. The younger one is, the more innate all of this is. I did not have a computer in my home until I was in high school. My children have been using them since they first learned to speak. The younger generations are becoming what

Richard Nolan, professor emeritus at Harvard Business School, refers to as "Digital Natives."[1] Technology is in their DNA, and the consequences are profound.

A similar evolutionary path can be tracked within corporations. Well into the 1980s technology leaders tended to follow a typical career track. They probably studied engineering at a university, they got their first jobs in some technology-centric business, and they worked their way up the corporate ladder. If they reached the apex of the technology department, they were nowhere close to being viewed as peers of other division leaders within the organization. To make matters worse, the tenure of the average chief information officer (CIO) was roughly two years. No wonder the acronym "CIO" was cynically referred to as "Career Is Over."

During this time, IT executives likely were overseeing the development of systems that assisted with "back-office" functions. They might have developed a homegrown accounting system; they might have developed systems to track employees' hours. These were important undertakings, to be sure, but CIOs tended not to garner invitations to the strategy-setting table at which the company's long-term vision was being discussed. They tended not to develop new innovations that would help the sales staff understand their customers better, to say nothing of systems that customers themselves would use. Frankly, customers did not expect to interact with the technology. There was no Internet; there were no self-serve gas stations or grocery checkout lanes. ATMs were barely known.

The late 1970s and early 1980s were a turning point. Personal computers gained in prominence. Answering machines became household necessities, and VCRs were used to record television programming or to watch movies. CIOs started to make inroads into adding recognizable value to the businesses in which they operated, though typically that value was in the form of cost-cutting. This was a time when automation was quickly replacing manual labor.

In the 1990s, a key innovation sparked the leap forward in the prominence of technology in everyday life: the Internet. Many people point to Netscape's initial public offering in August of 1995 as the watershed moment in this trend. The resources that the Internet offered increased the efficiency of research, putting a world of information at one's fingertips. Those who were connected—both individuals and companies—were advancing leaps and bounds beyond those who were not.

For a time in the late 1990s, I was a consultant in a firm that focused on eBusiness strategy. Our firm was composed of smart people who had one foot in business and the other in technology. It was an amazing time, as many industry leaders—companies that had operated successfully for decades—nervously watched an erosion of their market share to a new breed of companies. The most prominent example was Amazon stealing market share from older competitors such as Barnes & Noble and Borders Books. The term *Amazoned* entered into the popular lexicon, referring to a small, nimble, tech-centric company emerging out of nowhere to steal business from less nimble companies populated with Luddites.

Thus began the CIO revolution. All of a sudden, CEOs contemplating the ideal CIO began searching for technologists who had a strong head for business. A greater percentage of CIOs began to report to CEOs as opposed to CFOs or COOs. CIOs who were as comfortable with P&Ls as they were with 1s and 0s were given a seat at the strategy-setting table, influencing the business from a technology perspective. Likewise, CEOs began to think differently about technology, incorporating it into their long-term strategic plans.

Of course, there were many examples of what appeared to be changes in the rules governing business as a result of the explosion of eCommerce and eBusiness. One of my favorite stories from this period was about a group of three individuals who approached my firm asking for advice on an investment they had made. They had bought the domain name "cookies.com," and they wanted to know what sort of business they should create with it. Developing a company name and then going about determining the business to be in was definitely a new phenomenon. Of course, considering that the URL "business.com" was sold for $7.5 million, domain name speculation was a business in and of itself for a time. (Today, cookies.com links to a different site that does, in fact, sell cookies.)

It only made sense, therefore, that the dot-com bubble's burst in March of 2000 would lead to some cynicism about IT departments. For CEOs, CFOs, and COOs who had never embraced technology, this was a welcome comeuppance for the IT departments that they did not fully understand. However, for the new breed of CIOs who saw themselves as business leaders akin to the company's other division leaders, a shift had happened. There increasingly were examples of IT departments driving value to the top line and to the bottom line. IT would not prove such an easy victim for the chopping block as with previous economic downturns. CIOs had a seat at the strategic table and thus were able to articulate and defend their division's role. And there was now a wider appreciation of how technology could help a company survive and indeed prosper moving forward. Technology, in short, had become indispensable. As Bob Willett, CEO of Best Buy International and Enterprise CIO put it, "Nothing happens in a multilocated business unless it is driven through technology.... Technology is the agent of change, and your failure as a leader to understand how technology operates ... and how to take advantage of it, [means that] you are massively underestimating what it is that can be achieved."[2]

Fast forward to today, and we can see an emerging trend of CIOs becoming CEOs. In 2007, *Baseline* magazine ran a story about fifty-six tech executives who were climbing the ladder to become business executives, many of them CEOs.[3] This was a path that would have been unthinkable only a decade earlier. I predict that in a decade this number will have grown tremendously, and the reason is that technology is an inherent part of our daily experiences, as much as brushing our teeth and taking a shower are. Having an understanding of how technology can be used as a strategic weapon of the business therefore is a tremendously profitable skill. IT is a source of innovation, and CIOs who embrace the notion that they are stewards of innovation for the company can help spread innovation more broadly. When contemplating this topic, Willett noted that he thinks in the future CEOs will have been CIOs to a greater extent than chief financial officers or chief marketing officers. The reason he says, is due to the fact that "technology, unlike any other function, touches every single aspect of every business."[4]

Beyond CIOs' hallmark as innovators, they are also becoming known as problem solvers and executers. This is largely thanks to the increase both of IT budgets and of the complexity of the projects that IT undertakes. For these reasons, IT departments are becoming centers of excellence for project management. Thus there are a great number of broadly applicable skills that CIOs are building as their responsibilities grow.

CIOs have a historic opportunity today thanks to widespread recognition in business of the importance of technology. How can CIOs take advantage of this recognition? How can they deliver on the attendant expectations? Once they do deliver great results, how can they sustain high-level performance? And, perhaps most important for IT's success, how can CIOs demonstrate the value IT has added? This book provides a methodology for IT executives to achieve and sustain World Class IT performance. If many IT leaders already adhere to some of the principles contained herein, they likely focus on some to the exclusion of others. The key to World Class IT performance lies in monitoring the entire array of principles. And that, certainly, can be done by both leaders and laggards alike.

1

IT and Broader Company Vision

The modern IT department solves various problems across the business. As it does so, it is best positioned to suggest opportunities to cross-pollinate ideas or eliminate redundant efforts. It can also reinforce the business's strategic success by standardizing how the company communicates its objectives and needs.

Some IT departments have started to do this. Over the past ten years, successful ones have begun to measure their success through returns on IT investments and revenue enhancement for the business. In this chapter and throughout the book, I will identify some World Class IT departments who have led the way in creating value and helping their companies achieve true strategic change and success.

Why don't *more* corporate executives use IT as a strategic advantage? Among other reasons I will get into later, traditionally business and IT executives came from different backgrounds. The former had business degrees and learned the business on the "shop floor," focusing on the customers and catering to their needs. The IT folks tended to be technicians, often with master's degrees or Ph.D.s in engineering disciplines, who built systems to help the company be more productive. They did not get to know the customer, and in fact rarely linked their activities with either the corporate or business unit strategies. But this and other reasons no longer need to prevail.

Definition of World Class IT

What then does *World Class IT* mean? It is admittedly a loaded term. Everywhere around us, we see people suggesting that they offer "world-class service" or "world-class products" or "world-class employees." Often, these companies operate in a single geographic location, giving one the impression that they are like the baseball World Series, which despite its moniker only allows American teams to compete for the title "World Champion," save for the Toronto Blue Jays.

I will start with the potentially unsatisfying answer that there is no one definition of World Class IT. What works best for a multibillion-dollar multinational may not work well for a regionally focused startup. A company's size, scale of operations, geography, industry, and product and service mix will all affect how the company organizes itself. Moreover, companies in growth mode versus those that are cutting costs may operate differently. Industry leaders differ greatly from industry laggards.

That said, having consulted to a great number of companies that differ along most of the lines mentioned above, I can attest that there are some universal truths that can be applied to almost all of them. The best IT departments are populated with employees who understand the business that they are in. This is true not only of the CIO but also of the employees who are many layers beneath him or her in the organization chart. This may seem like a "no-brainer," but many if not most IT leaders do not take the care they should in exposing employees to the business. IT employees should understand how the company makes money and how it can save money, and understand the role that IT has in facilitating each of those processes. They should understand how the products and services work. IT departments that do not unlock the collective creativity of their staff by helping them understand how their department can affect the business are destroying potential value and keeping great ideas from percolating.

The leaders of the best IT departments constantly ask the question, "How can we improve?" On one of my first assignments introducing these concepts, my client was Harrah's Entertainment. Working with Harrah's was a daunting task because they were an unquestioned industry leader for which the IT department was considered one of the crown jewels of the company. The CIO at the time, John Boushy, was legendary, and several months thereafter, he would be succeeded by Tim Stanley, who would go on to also be a legendary CIO in his own right. John Boushy would go on to become CEO of Ameristar Casinos at least partially on the basis of his rare ability to translate business needs into creative IT solutions. Likewise, Stanley's success as a CIO would garner him added responsibilities including heading both Gaming Operations and Innovation for Harrah's in addition to his role as CIO, garnering the title CIO and SVP Gaming, Innovation and Technology. (Tim Stanley retired from Harrah's in January of 2009.)

At the outset of our collaboration, I was curious how well the IT leaders would take constructive criticism. Had all of the many articles that I had read in top business publications about the IT department and these two great IT minds caused them and their colleagues to believe that they could do no wrong? I was pleased to find that from the first day that I worked with them, they indicated that we had been brought in to help them understand how they could continue to improve. John and Tim requested that our analysis, insights, and recommendations come to them unfiltered, and that the shortest path to improvement be identified. I realized in short order why the department was so special.

The best IT departments also maintain dashboards of the entire department, to measure how all areas are performing on a regular basis. CEOs and CFOs have been doing this for a long time, but CIOs are more recent converts to instituting dashboards with comprehensive metrics. Some CIOs elect not to keep these metrics for the same reason that some people do not go to the doctor for regular checkups: they are worried about what they might find.

However, just as with one's personal health, if the right areas are evaluated, and the right metrics are kept, a problem can be identified early and a cure can be found before the problem becomes a terminal disease. Publishing dashboards and metrics provides positive pressure for the entire organization. Including the most important aspects of IT in the dashboards and conveying what the organization deems to be most important to measure will unlock the creative flow of ideas, as the entire department, and possibly even members of the organization as a whole, can develop new ideas on ways to improve.

The best IT departments also publish these dashboards and metrics for everyone to see. Broadcasting these metrics is equivalent to reaching a new land and burning the ships upon arrival: there is no going back. Sharing this information for a time and then not sharing it will lead everyone to suspect the worst. That said, the simple act of making the IT department's operation more transparent almost always is a move that will be admired, even if the baseline dashboards and metrics indicate that there is significant room for improvement.

The last characteristic that I have found typifying the best IT departments is a recognition that IT operates at a fortuitous position within the corporate structure. IT departments have relationships with each of the other business units such as marketing, sales, finance, human resources, and product specific divisions that differ company by company. Although human resources has a relationship with each of the other business units because they are involved in recruiting, hiring, training, and firing people, and finance has a similar relationship because it has to evaluate how each business unit proposes to spend the company's limited resources, IT departments have the opportunity to weave themselves into the fabric of the business unit's planning processes. They deliver technologies to each of the other areas, and if they manage the demand that the business has for IT solutions appropriately, they should see where there are needs and demands from each business unit that may overlap. Moreover, they have the opportunity to understand how an investment proposed by one area of the business might have implications for other parts of the business. This requires that IT leaders be business savvy, drawing out the right kind of information from colleagues in the business units while creating enough value to be asked to engage in these sorts of conversations on a regular basis.

There are two examples that I would like to provide for this last point. The first is significant, as it shows that an IT department can operate at a world-class level of performance within a company that is not performing well, and therefore it can play a large role in turning the company around. The second highlights that IT's advantageous perch within the corporate structure provides the CIO and others in the department the opportunity to exercise influence beyond IT's traditional role for the betterment of the company as a whole.

Example: IT's Saving Role at United Airlines

Nirup Krishnamurthy managed the IT department of an organization not in growth mode but rather in the throes of Chapter 11 restructuring—United Airlines. Due to a confluence of factors, from a bear market to increased fuel prices to decreased business and leisure travel to ticket prices reaching ten-year lows to the effects of the terrorist attacks on September 11, United was in dire straits. United cut costs in all areas of the company in an attempt to restructure its way back to health. Krishnamurthy's IT department experienced significant cuts, which forced him to develop a better means of understanding how to prioritize the company's needs. He worked directly with the business executives to do so and developed the following strategic themes:

- Cost leadership
- Customer experience

- Revenue optimization
- IT infrastructure
- Shared services optimization
- Safety and compliance
- Employee engagement

For example, to adhere to the customer experience theme, each business unit proposed ways in which it could enhance the customer experience, and, working with Krishnamurthy and his team, prioritized the resulting ideas.

Even though United's IT investment approach came as a result of extreme circumstances, by pushing the business to prioritize, setting a strategic framework to manage demands of IT, Krishnamurthy and the IT department can claim a healthy amount of credit for assisting United Airlines in emerging from Chapter 11 bankruptcy protection and returning to profitability. As Pete McDonald, EVP and chief operating officer at the time, recounted, "We realized that using IT would be a critical component to mitigating the issues we faced."[1] Although IT is often among the first budgets cut during difficult financial times, CIOs who realize the important strategic position that they have in the company can be part of the solution to the problems that help the company turn around.

Of course, not so surprisingly, there are many leading IT departments that operate within industry leaders, as shown in the second example.

Example: IT at McKesson as Corporate Glue

At McKesson Corporation, executive vice president, chief information officer, and chief technology officer Randy Spratt inherited a challenged organization when he joined the company through its acquisition of HBOC in 1999. McKesson realized that it should be getting more value from its IT department, and Spratt was tasked with enhancing the department's value. Spratt engaged the business in a new way, asking business unit leaders for their objectives and their needs, and having them participate on governance councils during which they would not only present their needs and requests but also listen to their peers submit their own. This facilitated a great deal of cross-business-unit learning that had not existed previously.

As a result, McKesson executives began to appreciate that IT was becoming the glue that helped the organization stick together in ways it had not in the past. As the business units began to understand more about each other, IT drove them to eliminate redundant efforts, identified where synergies existed that did not occur to the business units because they had previously operated in silos, and generally increased the amount of cross-pollination of ideas and business opportunities across the corporation.

When McKesson executives decided to merge with Per Se Technologies for $1.8 billion in November 2006, Spratt played an integral role. Like all acquisitions, this one had implications for many different functions, from HR to finance to various parts of the operations of both companies. In a two-day session, Spratt brought together the sixteen managers who oversaw the sixteen work streams identified for the merger integration, to share their plans and make adjustments so that the whole plan fit together. As the integration proceeded, progress was charted online so that all relevant constituents could track where the project stood.[2]

Just a few years ago, the thought of the IT department leading a corporation's efforts in a merger would have been considered unrealistic. How could IT people possibly understand the needs of the various business functions, and how could IT reconcile the sometimes competing interests that must be weighed during the integration of two companies? These and other objections would have prevented IT from playing the prominent role it now plays at McKesson.

As the president of Metis Strategy, I have been fortunate to advise a wide range of CIOs and CTOs, many of whom have worked or fought their way to their companies' strategy-setting tables by demonstrating that IT can be a strategic weapon and a source of competitive advantage. These executives are proactive in offering advice to the business rather than simply waiting for orders to fill. It is no accident that business executives at these companies now recognize the critical value that IT can add.

Five Principles of World Class IT

Expanding the value of IT begins with (but will not end with) ensuring that your IT department is truly world class.

On the basis of our experience in working with World Class IT organizations, my colleagues and I have come to recognize five principles that can ensure that the IT department contributes all it can to the company. The principles are as follows.

Principle 1: Recruit, train, and retain World Class IT employees. Without the right people, the IT organization will have little chance for ultimate success. It is essential that the company take care of its people, make them feel part of something that is bigger than themselves, and inspire them to think of their relationship with the company with a long-term perspective.

Principle 2: Build and maintain a robust IT infrastructure. IT organizations that do not have a reliable infrastructure are caught "fighting fires" day in and day out. Proper infrastructure allows employees to think creatively and proactively about new solutions that may help the business. By getting this principle right, the organization can carve out more time and attention to focus on adding value for the business and for IT itself.

Principle 3: Manage projects and portfolios effectively. Having a sound software-development lifecycle (SDLC) that is used by all areas of IT is critical to ensuring that new ideas are brought to bear quickly, reliably, and consistently. Having a sound project management and portfolio management process ensures that projects are prioritized, and that limited time, resources, and funds are focused on the most important initiatives. Doing all of this in a way that is easy to convey to business partners ensures that the business understands IT, and that it does its part to guarantee that the right projects are chosen and that they remain on track to fruition.

Principle 4: Ensure partnerships within the IT department and with the business. With the right people, reliable infrastructure, and processes that will allow projects to be delivered in a creative and timely fashion, the IT department will have the credibility to gain a seat at the business's strategy-setting table. Once it has, associates in the department at all levels can act as peers and advisers to the business, both by reacting to the needs of the business with creative solutions to meet those needs and by being mindful of how trends in IT can have an impact on the business, thereby helping the business realize how it can best leverage technology even before the business has articulated its needs.

Principle 5: Develop a collaborative relationship with external partners. With the clear understanding of the strategic sources of competitive advantage created by principles 1 through 4, the business can then put more thought into which areas of the company are best managed by someone outside of the company. This fifth principle deals with understanding how to forge relationships with external partners that will provide them incentives to overperform, and to bring fresh, new, creative ideas to the table rather than to simply fulfill the letter of the contract and nothing more. Although the decision to engage external partners can have unintended long-term ramifications and therefore should not be made lightly, there is no doubt that outsourcing is an important weapon in the IT executive's arsenal.

Figure 1.1 shows the broad relationship of the principles to each other. They are depicted in a continuous cycle because once improvements are made relative to each of the five principles in

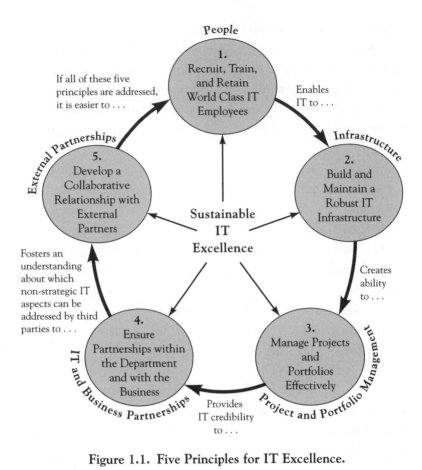

Figure 1.1. Five Principles for IT Excellence.

their appropriate order, the next phase of the cycle is enhanced. For example, the figure starts with people, but the next four phases make the company a more attractive place to work. This makes hiring and retaining employees easier, and the process therefore comes back again to further improvements in terms of your people.

Each principle has corresponding metrics and processes that can then be put in place to ensure the company's ultimate success. The principles are not entirely new, nor are they hard to follow. The truth is that most great IT organizations do some of these things well and other things not so well. The idea of this methodology is to monitor *all* five together.

What This Book Will Do

The next five chapters of this book will cover these principles one by one, breaking them down into greater detail and providing examples of companies that are operating at a high level relative to the topic principle. The chapters are guides for IT and business executives alike in understanding what it takes to achieve World Class IT performance. The five chapters will also convey ideas that these companies have pursued that represent new thinking in the realm of IT management.

At the conclusion of each chapter, I have provided suggested metrics for CIOs to use to monitor performance. It is critical that the IT department measure and communicate its performance. I have noted two levels of metrics for each of the subprinciples: introductory metrics and advanced metrics. Note that there may be other metrics that should be added or supplemented in place to make them as relevant as possible to each company. That said, in each chapter I have attempted to state metrics in terms to make them as broadly applicable as possible.

It is also important to note that not all metrics can be instituted. If the baseline of each metric cannot be established because the data are too difficult or expensive to obtain, then I do not suggest making unreasonable investments of time and effort to be sure that all of the suggested metrics are put in place. That said, if these metrics are unrealistic, alternatives must be found. It is not acceptable to avoid metrics.

When instituting metrics, we advise clients to think about the acronym "SMART." This stands for the following:

- *Specific:* A metric is specific if it is clearly defined and the ownership of the metric is clear. It is important that individuals be assigned to each of the metrics.

- *Measurable:* A baseline or a starting point must be established for each metric. The desired improvement should also be measurable. Without both of these, then the metric is not useful.

- *Actionable:* This requires that the company or the department (in the case of this book, typically the IT department) have control over the metric. This is important so that IT can influence its outcome. If the IT department does not have direct contact with external customers, and yet metrics for customer satisfaction are tied to IT's success, there may be a disconnect. Either direct ties to the customer must be established or a new metric should be implemented.

- *Relevant:* When defining metrics, one must consider significance to the IT department. The defined metrics that are met must truly improve the performance of the department. Metrics also must be value-based. An IT department should not be judged as successful on the basis of the number of projects that it implements. Instead, it should be judged on the value derived from those projects, and whether they were delivered on time, on budget, and within the defined scope.

- *Timely:* Data for the metrics must be available in a time frame that enables them to be acted upon. If the data are not readily available, then the necessary improvements will not be timely as well, which defeats the purpose of the metrics in the first place.

In addition to assigning an owner to each metric, as mentioned, a target needs to be established for each metric. Not defining ultimate success is like driving without a destination in mind.

It is also important to note that the fewer metrics the better. Just as the IT department should not have too many objectives in its strategic plan for fear that it will not provide a filtering process, likewise, having too many metrics will convolute the process and not foster the focus that good metrics should provide.

Projects and other initiatives should eventually be tied to these metrics to ensure that the improvements are being made. If the department defines metrics, but does not take action to improve upon them, then it goes without saying that the metrics will not be achieved.

Last, the metrics should be reevaluated at least annually if not more frequently. Changes to the company, changes to the industry, or macroeconomic changes may cause a need to rethink some of the metrics.

In closing, I should mention that I have avoided dealing with trends of the day in this book. Where I have provided examples from companies, I believe them to be examples that are worthy of emulation, even if they may need to be tailored to different industries, geographies, and company sizes. A goal of this book is to identify universal principles that are more timeless and less trendy. A critique of many IT books is that much of what they cover is irrelevant soon after they are published by virtue of the pace of technology change. I don't mean to suggest that the subprinciples defined herein will not change, or that new ones will not need to be added. That is likely, but I believe that the majority of them have staying power, and IT departments and the companies that they operate in can institute this framework without fear that it will be rendered irrelevant soon thereafter.

2

Principle 1: Recruit, Train, and Retain World Class IT People

Your organization needs World Class IT people. Before getting into recruiting, training, and retaining them, let's think about two common contemporary concerns: the need for flexibility among workers and the need to keep them accountable.

The Future of Work

In 2005, Gregor Bailar, then the executive vice president and chief information officer of Capital One, realized that the development of a new corporate campus in Richmond, Virginia, provided the company an opportunity to think differently about the way in which employees worked. Collaborating with the facilities organization and human resources, Bailar developed a new approach that he termed the "Future of Work." Bailar gave up an office and suggested that others do the same. Instead of assigned offices and cubicles, Capital One developed an open office environment with few walls and plenty of sunlight. People were encouraged to sit in teams, so that colleagues who had reason to collaborate on a regular basis could readily do so. As Bailar describes it, "Facilities folks and the HR folks saw that buildings were not being used in the same way that they had been. Offices and cubicles remained empty while people crowded into the few conference rooms that were available. Managers and employees were having a different relationship because employees were going from one project to the next, perhaps many in one year. There was a change in the way that people actually worked on projects."[1]

To Bailar's and other executives' delight, this decision ended up paying big dividends for the company. Innovation actually increased as a result of consolidating teams in this fashion. Collaboration was enhanced, meetings were made more efficient, and, ultimately, productivity and employee satisfaction rose. In addition, the company was able to save money on real estate, as less office space was necessary, and the paper and document management costs also decreased due to the implementation of better electronic data storage since people literally had less space to store papers without dedicated offices and cubicles.

Technology was a large part of the story. To ensure the people could work in such a flexible fashion, they needed to have reliable wi-fi connections so that their PCs would be operable anywhere. Voice over Internet Protocol (VoIP) phones were put in place. Also, the improvements in document management allowed people to access information almost from anywhere.

This is a trend that is starting to take shape to a greater degree, but will likely increase as more companies look to find ways to enhance the productivity of their staffs while also lowering costs. This is a change that IT can help push that will help both the top line (through greater innovation) and the bottom line (through cost savings).

Best Buy's ROWE

Best Buy, the electronics retailing leader, also provides employees with alternatives to the office environment, and has had measurable results. All of Best Buy's corporate employees and even some of the store employees are allowed to work when they want and where they want so long as they deliver the results that they have promised.

Because at Best Buy results are what matter most, the program is known as ROWE—Results Only Work Environment.

As the CIO of Best Buy and CEO of Best Buy International, Bob Willett has led the development of the infrastructure that helps ensure that the ROWE approach to people works. Willett's role in ROWE is not to be underestimated, and his task isn't simple. For thousands of employees to work wherever they wish for large stretches of time requires an especially flexible and reliable IT infrastructure. (We'll be saying much more in general about infrastructure in the next chapter, "Principle 2.") There are special security issues to be considered when thousands of employees can access Best Buy's most sensitive information from outside the company's walls. Collaborative tools had to be created to make ROWE possible. Perhaps most important to note here is that someone must maintain the metrics that determine the results (the first letter in ROWE, after all) when using this technology. Willett has succeeded in these things, and results in fact have been positive. Two years after the program's creation, ROWE had increased worker productivity by 35 percent in those divisions that had implemented it.[2]

A ROWE approach is best suited to employees who work on independent projects, and who can work without supervision. It requires that assignments and the expected results be very clearly delineated and understood. Generally speaking, one area that companies must monitor if they are thinking about ROWE is that relatively junior employees often don't yet have the maturity and discipline to effectively work from home with regularity. For many junior staff, face time matters. They typically require more mentoring, and they may not as readily feel as though they are part of something that is bigger than themselves.

The point of this introduction is to show that virtual workplaces and outcome-based management are two major ways that IT can be used to acquire and maximize the output of world-class talent.

Ten Subprinciples of the "People" Principle

Let's look now systematically at how an IT department can go about "recruiting, training, and retaining World Class IT people."

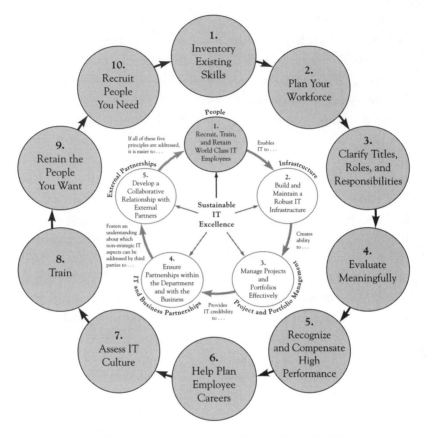

Figure 2.1. Ten Subprinciples for a World Class IT Workforce.

Figure 2.1 shows ten subprinciples for achieving these goals. As IT leaders strive to create the world-class company of today, it is equally important to ensure that junior staff develop the skills they will need to lead the world-class company of the future.

Subprinciple 1. Inventory Existing Skills

To efficiently allocate talent or determine what skill gaps exist, you need first to understand what skills your employees already have. To begin, define the sorts of skills that you will need, such as the following (in this illustrative, not exhaustive list):

- Technical skills
  - Programming languages
  - Hardware and software development capabilities
  - Application programming and development
  - Database management
  - Network or server administration
  - Security administration
  - Systems administration
  - Information technology administrative support
  - Telecommunications
- Management skills
  - Accreditation such as PMI certification
  - Facilities management
  - Configuration management
- Business skills
  - Finance
  - Accounting
  - Marketing
  - General management
  - Client support services
- Other skills
  - Languages spoken

Optimally, these skills should be listed and described as explicitly as possible on a standardized online form that will allow employees to see the skills that are currently tabulated, so that they can begin their self-assessment. They can also begin to think about which skills they might want to acquire. For instance, if Web 2.0 skills are important, note these, and ask people to provide examples. Or if the business is about to expand to China, it would be important to list "languages" as a necessary skill, and specify either "Mandarin" or "Cantonese."

In addition, Eric Lundquist, in his blog *Upfront*, has identified the following skills necessary for entry-level employees:[3]

1. Ethics and morals
2. Critical thinking and problem solving
3. Collaboration/teams
4. Problem solving
5. Communication: Oral
6. Communication: Written
7. User relationship management
8. Creativity/innovation
9. Managing expectations
10. Programming/application development
11. Decision making
12. Functional area knowledge
13. Project leadership
14. Database
15. System analysis

It is striking how essentially all of these could apply to most other parts of the business beyond information management or IT functions. This is also clearly the case when one surveys Lundquist's list of skills for mid-level hires:[4]

1. Ethics and morals
2. Collaboration and teams
3. Critical thinking and problem solving
4. Communication: Oral and written
5. Project leadership
6. Managing expectations and user relationship management
7. Decision making

8. Business analysis

9. Creativity and innovation

10. Budgets, leadership, and project integration

Again, we see that the area of IT looks a lot more like the business these days, and this is definitely a good sign.

Subprinciple 2. Plan Your Workforce

After the skill inventory is in place, it is important for IT leaders to contemplate where the organization is going and what skill sets will become increasingly important in the future. This workforce planning exercise is critical to define the gulf between the current state versus the desired future state for skills. An important input to this is the business and IT strategy. What does the direction of the company suggest in terms of IT skills that will be necessary? For instance, if the company is on the verge of making a push onto the web, then clearly web development skills will grow in importance. Likewise, a robust analysis of which systems will gain in prominence versus those that will likely retire will help the organization draw conclusions about which skills are essential and which are likely to become less relevant or even irrelevant.

Subprinciple 3. Clarify Titles, Roles, and Responsibilities

After the inventory of current skills is tabulated, and the list of needed skills is contemplated, you should establish clear titles, roles, and responsibilities. This is a relatively easy step that mitigates a lot of frustration. Poor descriptions of titles, roles, and responsibilities makes it much more difficult for employees, especially high performers, to understand what they must do in order to advance in the organization. It is critical to unlock the ambition of one's employees by demarcating the differences between levels within different skill sets and across the IT department.

This may seem like it is so obvious as to not be worth mentioning. You might be surprised to learn that many of the companies with which I have worked have had challenges in this area. The reasons include a lack of HR engagement in defining technology roles, which tend to be different from roles in other parts of the organization, to the fact that, like technology, best practices in role definition change quickly, and therefore can become stale quickly as well.

Clarity on this front can go a long way toward improving employee satisfaction and retaining key talent that can, in turn, play a vital role in the future health of the company.

Subprinciple 4. Evaluate Meaningfully

Defining clear roles and responsibilities enables meaningful evaluations. You need these in order to provide detailed constructive feedback about each employee's strengths and weaknesses. Managers must take the time to evaluate the performance of those who report to them, and to speak with others who have worked with them. All feedback should be clearly documented. The evaluation should have a standard set of questions, and should establish the employee as either a high, average, or low performer. This type of evaluation can then be used in determining skill gaps and workforce needs for the organization.

Also have employees assess themselves. All employees should be required to provide a personal assessment. The framework for assessment should be established by the employee upon hiring, by having him or her answer the following questions:

- What are your goals for the one-, three-, and five-year time horizons?
- What do you believe are your greatest strengths?
- What skills do you hope to acquire?
- What do you believe are your primary weaknesses?

Having employees establish their own baselines allows for a more meaningful evaluation, allowing them to judge their progress according to their own ambitions.

Subprinciple 5. Recognize and Compensate High Performance

There are essentially five ways in which an employee can be recognized:

- Salary
- Bonus payment
- Recognition in front of peers
- Increased responsibility
- Assignment of company-critical tasks

Compensation and recognition can be tricky for managers because people are motivated in different ways. Many of our clients establish employee recognition programs that are similar to loyalty programs for customers. Just as American Express realizes that some clients are motivated by "cash back" and others prefer frequent flyer miles as their "reward," likewise, companies too should work to understand what motivates their employees.

I recall working with a high-performing project manager at a client organization whose bosses regularly praised him in front of his colleagues for his good work. Unfortunately, when I asked him how he felt about this recognition, he said he was embarrassed to be called out in front of his colleagues. What had been intended to be a very positive moment was exactly the opposite. Thankfully, it did not cause him to stop doing good work, but it wasn't how to motivate him. Had superiors asked what he wanted, he would have said he preferred more private recognition, perhaps through a mention on the departmental email that went out each month with updates on goings on across the department.

A particular challenge is trying to recognize the accomplishments of IT infrastructure workers. This group often gets overlooked because it is generally called only when problems occur. Rarely is "John" recognized in a monthly newsletter or company intranet because "the systems that John is responsible for did not fail at all in the last quarter." However, we all know what John hears when systems fail. We need to reward him when they don't.

Encouragingly, IT employees are often among the best compensated, because their skills are highly transferrable and increasingly essential. You should regularly benchmark companies in your general locale to be certain that IT compensation packages are competitive. Of course, pay special attention to the compensation and recognition of high performers, who often know that they are good and will not sit idly by if their superior work does not translate to superior compensation.

Subprinciple 6. Help Plan Employee Careers

IT departments also need to develop a substantial career-planning capability. Although many of my clients believe that it is the individual's responsibility to plan his or her own career, the best people may not know how to think about their career strategically and accrue the right skills along the way. New employees are especially disadvantaged in not knowing what the current leaders did to get to their positions. Employers risk losing new employees by not letting them know of the opportunities before them.

One way to ensure employee growth and development is to establish one-on-one mentoring with senior colleagues. All employees should be encouraged to pick out informal mentors with whom they can build trusted relationships and seek advice. In my own career, I received invaluable advice from a friend's father who indicated that his own rise in the business world was largely due to finding the right mentors, and learning from their successes and their mistakes. Even today I seek the counsel of people in comparable fields in order to get advice during critical transitional phases in my firm.

Another important step in nurturing employee development is to establish a clear technical track as well as a managerial track to more senior positions. Although management skills and experience are important, you do not want to lose highly technically skilled people because they do not acquire management skills. Define a track that provides strong technologists with a reason to stay and advance within the company, rather than essentially being forced to go elsewhere.

Subprinciple 7. Assess IT Culture

Culture is "the set of beliefs, values, and norms, together with symbols that represents the unique character of an organization, and provides the context for action in it and by it."[5] In many organizations today, this is believed to be a "soft" topic that is difficult to measure success against. Savvy IT departments and companies more generally have come to realize that there are hard benefits such as increased employee satisfaction and reduced attrition. Defining the IT culture should help provide a broader context to the jobs that each member of the department does. It should also provide a better vision for people who are new to the organization.

There are many reasons why an organization should assess its culture. Consider the following scenarios:

- A new CIO has been hired and, for him- or herself as much as for the team, he or she wants to understand the company's culture.

- The IT organization is a leading division of the company and wishes to define and formalize what makes it special.

- The IT organization is lagging behind and wishes to define its culture as part of highlighting its current values to itself and to its business partners.

The first step in understanding an organization's culture is to capture the key themes and concepts of the existing culture by conducting a survey that assesses the perspectives, perceptions, and expectations of the organization. The survey should be useful in helping to highlight areas of alignment and misalignment as well as areas of opportunity by leveraging relevant external "best practices." Once the survey is completed and analyzed, the IT leader should circle back with key players and stakeholders to validate and refine findings, delve deeper into select critical issues, and recommend how the evolving IT organizational culture can best be nurtured.

Specific deliverables should result:

1. A list of individuals who are well-suited to serve as custodians and proselytizers of the cultural change process

2. Success measures that will permit the organization to continuously gauge the impact and the achievements of the cultural change efforts

3. A revised, IT-organization-specific cultural survey to be used on a regular basis

4. A communication strategy and a universal core message to shape organizational culture

5. An analysis and progress report based on multiple surveys and cultural audits undertaken across the duration of the first year of instituting the new culture

6. Formulation of a revised and long-term "target state" of the organizational culture

7. Suggested tools and mechanics to promote ongoing cultural evolution

8. Profiles of internal best practices and quick-wins of the early phase(s) of the cultural change effort to promote continuing change and facilitate best-practices sharing

9. More detailed opportunity gap analysis and recommendations on how to close those gaps

Subprinciple 8. Train

Practically all the principles mentioned so far are implemented through training. Training is the way in which new employees are introduced to the IT organization, how skills are acquired, and how practices are shared more broadly. Although training costs time and money, employees who don't receive regular training become stagnant and bored. That is why some CEOs such as Phaneesh Murthy of IT outsourcing company iGATE puts all new employees through three-and-a-half months of training to familiarize them with the company and to standardize terminology and expectations.[6] This is expensive, but it also is invaluable.

The key to training is ensuring that it is relevant. General training is good for onboarding people. All people should know about the company history, its culture, and the like. After that, training should be tailored to the needs of the individual based on their tenure, their positions, and their ambitions.

As the company engages outside vendors to take over aspects of the IT department (a topic we will cover in more detail in Chapter Six), it is necessary that baked into these contracts is the training of the IT department's (if not other department's) employees. Large outsourcing firms often have a great many areas in which they have expertise. It is easy and cheap to insist that they include among their services training days on topics that are of interest to the company and the IT department.

One other recent phenomenon is the mobility of training. With so many people traveling with work, or operating in a virtual workspace, it is important that many aspects of training be made available 24/7, so that employees can choose to take training on their own schedules and in the location of their choosing.

Subprinciple 9. Retain the People You Want

A good retention strategy requires organizations to assess their entire staff and determine which employees will grow and develop into the next generation of leaders. General Electric famously divides its employees into three groups.

Jack Welch introduced this concept in the 2000 "Annual Report to GE Share Owners." He said, "We break our population down into three categories: the top 20%, the high-performing 70%, and the bottom 10%." He went on to explain that top 10 percent must be "loved and nurtured in the soul and wallet," while the bottom 10 percent should be removed.[7]

Counseling out the low performers is important, and it actually plays a large role in helping retention for those who remain, as they recognize that there are ramifications for consistent underperformance. This then makes room for new talent. If ambitious and hard-working IT staff do not see action taken against consistently low performers, their energy will wane, and they may take their ambition and hard work elsewhere.

Subprinciple 10. Recruit People You Need

Recruiting is, of course, the lifeblood of any organization. It is important that new people join the team, offer new skills, share relevant experiences, and help you to look at old problems afresh. Like technology, skills can become outdated quickly. New IT employees help ensure that the organization remains competitive and up to date on the latest ideas and skills.

Metrics

As the ROWE example earlier suggests, results are important. Whether a company is ready to institutionalize the level of flexibility that Best Buy has or not, measuring how the IT department is doing is of the utmost importance.

The metrics of the subprinciples related to people tend to be "softer" in nature. They tend to be metrics that are based on surveys of employees or surveys of managers or business partners as they relate to the performance of IT employees. Most companies already have surveys of these kinds in place, but in order to institute these metrics, additional questions may need to be devised and added to the surveys.

Table 2.1. Metrics for Recruiting, Training, and Retaining World Class IT People.

Subprinciple	Introductory Metrics	Advanced Metrics
Inventory Existing Skills	• Percentage of employees with documented skills	• Skill inventory maintained and skill inventory used • Ratio between skills used and skills documented
Plan Your Workforce	• The ratio between planned positions and open positions • The ratio between planned positions and current positions • Frequency of workforce planning • The time horizon for workforce planning	• Percentage of positions mapped to long-term strategy • Percentage of positions mapped to infrastructure roadmap
Clarify Titles, Roles, and Responsibilities	• Alignment between employee evaluation criteria and titles, roles, and responsibilities • Optimize the number of titles, roles, and responsibilities	• Employee satisfaction related to roles and titles

Table 2.1.   Metrics for Recruiting, Training, and Retaining World Class IT People. (*Continued*)

Subprinciple	Introductory Metrics	Advanced Metrics
Evaluate Meaning-fully	• Percentage of IT employee evaluations submitted on time • Percentage improvement in mean evaluation score • Percentage improvement in median evaluation score • Employee satisfaction related to evaluation	• Percentage of actions taken related to evaluations (such as training, advancement, demotion, salary adjustments) • Ratio between evaluation criteria and titles, roles, and responsibilities
Recognize and Compensate High Performance	• Average bonus as compared to total bonus value for IT employees (compared to similarly salaried employees in other BUs) • Percentage of employees eligible for bonuses • Percentage of employees promoted annually • Compensation validated as comparable to other companies in industry and geography	• Average deviation from average bonus for high and low performers • Number and frequency of noncompensation awards given

Table 2.1. *(Continued)*

Subprinciple	Introductory Metrics	Advanced Metrics
Help Plan Employee Careers	• Percentage of employees with approved career plans • Percentage of annual career development plan goals met • Percentage of employees with mentors	• Percentage of advancements per review cycle • Percentage of employees advancing aligned with career plan • Percentage of open positions filled internally through promotion
Assess IT Culture	• Percentage improvement in employee understanding of culture attributes	• Percentage improvement in employee satisfaction based on agreement with culture attributes • Reduced attrition after the institutionalization of the cultural analysis
Train	• Alignment between hours of training required and hours of training accomplished per employee • Number of required and voluntary training courses offered	• Alignment of training activities with titles, roles, and responsibilities • Alignment of training activities with individual career plans

Table 2.1.   Metrics for Recruiting, Training, and Retaining World
Class IT People. (*Continued*)

Subprinciple	Introductory Metrics	Advanced Metrics
Train, cont'd.	• Percentage of IT employees fulfilling training requirement • Percentage of IT employees attending voluntary training courses • Retention rate of new hires in first ninety days • Instructor performance scores • Post-training survey scores • Ratio of number of employees compared to capacity to train those employees	• Percentage of employee-driven training as opposed to company-driven training • Average cost per training event (per hour for e-learning or per day for in person) • Degree (percentage) of availability of training at product or services launch • Training facility utilization • Instructor utilization • Training recruiting and turnover ratios • Percentage of training program utilization during X period
Retain the People You Want	• Percentage of voluntary turnover of IT staff • Percentage of involuntary turnover of IT staff	• Percentage of IT employees lost to other companies versus other departments in the company

Table 2.1.   (Continued)

Subprinciple	Introductory Metrics	Advanced Metrics
	• Percentage of "top performer" turnover	
	• Average tenure of IT staff	
Recruit People You Need	• Average time to hire	• Percentage of new hires with high performance review scores six months after hire
	• Response rate relative to open positions	
	• Percentage of hires hired by "need date"	
	• Yield on offers	

Connecting IT's People Work with Its Greater Company Role

When I speak to IT executives about these "people" principles, some point out that IT departments can't act alone, that HR must be involved in many of these decisions in order to ensure that they are enacted correctly, and that the business must make similar changes in order for IT to change. If the IT department must wait for these other departments, and accept that change is not within its own power to achieve, then this speaks volumes about the weakness of IT in the corporate structure. When that happens, the IT department should push its partners in other areas of the business to ensure the positive change is enacted across the organization. There is nothing that says that IT should not be a leader when it comes to the ways in which the company recruits, trains, and retains people.

Principle 2: Build and Maintain a Robust IT Infrastructure

Before embarking on a journey of the dos and don'ts of IT infrastructure, it is important to define the term. I define infrastructure as IT hardware, software, data, components, systems, applications, and the service desk that supports them. Other definitions that I have seen include the people associated with IT, but as you will have noted in the previous chapter, we have separated them out.

Given that point of clarification, note that the "infrastructure principle" is the most IT-centric of the five we will cover in this book. This is the topic that non-IT employees may not understand despite the fact that they are accustomed to using the infrastructure when they use email, log their hours, or access client information through a database. They understand graphical user interfaces, they understand that when they hit the power button on the PC that it should turn on, they understand the systems that they use on a day-to-day basis, but there is a good chance that non-IT employees do not understand infrastructure at a deeper level. These things need to be explained in terms that others can understand. Only this can ensure the company's willingness to invest appropriately, mitigating risks and keeping systems reliable. After working and speaking with a wide variety of CIOs and heads of infrastructure for major IT departments, I have concluded that superior IT departments are those that are able to translate IT infrastructure into terms and categories that make sense to IT's business partners. Lesser IT organizations operate in a vacuum—insufficiently explaining infrastructure performance and needs to the business at large. In the end, the IT department suffers from this as much as the overall business. Remember that IT employees ultimately are tasked with making sense of the infrastructure hairball that results when obsolete systems aren't retired and replaced by newer, more reliable systems. When the IT department puts off communicating with other departments, complexity often increases to the breaking point.

It is also important to prioritize infrastructure to understand which are the most important components of infrastructure for the business. Those are the attributes of infrastructure that should be maintained most thoroughly, and should be streamlined to the greatest extent possible. Hilton Hotels offers an example of a complex IT infrastructure. Hilton acquired Promus Hotel Corporation in 2000, and in so doing, purchased a property management technology called System21. System21 had been developed under the stewardship of Promus EVP and CIO Tim Harvey. Most hotel companies have different systems for reservation management, property management, CRM, revenue management, forecast and content management, and the like. These are the strategic systems for a hotel company, and therefore are some of the most important aspects of hotel companies' infrastructure. If these go down, revenue may be lost. With System21, which was renamed OnQ after the acquisition by Hilton, the company had one solution that managed all of these components. Therefore, whereas most other companies have a disparate web of infrastructure in managing these various components, Hilton has consolidated the infrastructure, making it easier to bring a new hotel online with all of Hilton's standard systems. This is a tremendous advantage as the company continues to grow. As Harvey puts it, "the integrated components of OnQ are about knowing the customer, selling the product at the right price, and executing the stay, supported by a full-scale approach to business intelligence that allows for timely decisions and critical marketing functions. With 62 percent of our sales and reservations coming from OnQ components, and 40 percent from our Hilton Honors program, OnQ's ability to share customer data consistently across all touch points will continue to play a major role for the Hilton Family."[1]

Beyond explaining things effectively, the key to running an efficient and highly available IT infrastructure is to listen to one's business partners. Their guidance will provide indications as to the following:

- Which are the mission critical systems?
  - This then translates into determining which need to be most available and therefore monitored, refreshed, and maintained accordingly.
- Which systems are relevant, or becoming less relevant?
  - This offers a path to potential big savings, especially if there are systems that can replace them or if they can be retired without replacement.
- What new infrastructure will be necessary to support the business's vision for the future?

IT infrastructure is a hot topic in many companies, as it is often considered an area that is ripe for outsourcing. (I'll say more about this under principle 5.) This has yielded mixed results when companies outsource for the wrong reasons. One commonly cited reason is costs. Although costs savings have been achieved from outsourcing infrastructure, often no savings result. The better reason to outsource is to enhance the reliability of systems. The usual-suspect outsourced-service organizations (IBM, Infosys, EDS, and the like) that succeed in abetting a wide range of organizations are able to use their experience across many different companies to ensure that systems will be reliable. What is sometimes lost, however, is flexibility.

David Richter has been the head of infrastructure at multiple *Fortune* 500 companies. He is currently Vice President of IT Services—Infrastructure Solutions at Kimberly-Clark. When I asked him about how best to think about outsourcing, he said, "What I have found works much better for infrastructure is what I define as a co-source model where an offshore partner is used for Level 1 and Level 2 engineering to gain the benefits of labor arbitrage and Levels 3 and 4 are kept in house to support projects. Thus the company benefits by keeping critical knowledge and capabilities in-house while reducing costs for the low-level engineering and service desk work."

Another peculiarity about infrastructure is the tendency for the departments that lead IT infrastructure to develop "infrastructure heroes." Infrastructure is peculiar in that it is typically noticed only when things go wrong. As a result, it becomes a part of the IT department that is not recognized sufficiently for things going right (such as hardware and systems performing as they are supposed to) even if it takes a great deal of effort to ensure that they do. This peculiarity can lead to the development of people who thrive on fighting fires and are bored by stable environments that fail to showcase their heroics. Be sure that metrics do not provide the incentive to have buggy code. The IT department should not base success on number of bugs found, but on having the fewest number of bugs and the long-term quality of the technology.

Seven Subprinciples of Infrastructure

To gain some ground in maintaining and operating an efficient IT infrastructure, there are seven subprinciples that can be followed, shown in Figure 3.1.

Subprinciple 1. Create an Infrastructure Roadmap

Just as in the previous "people" discussion a skills inventory was the first step toward establishing performance excellence with people, so creating an infrastructure roadmap is the first, critical step for

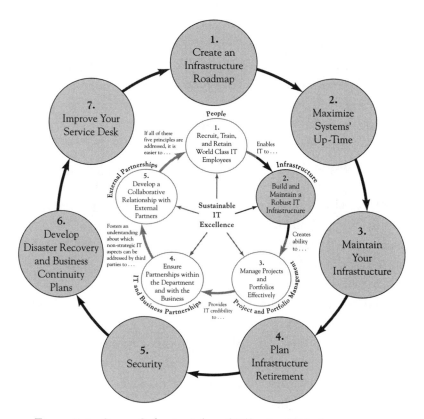

Figure 3.1. Seven Subprinciples of Effective IT Infrastructure.

infrastructure. You need to know the starting point, from which you can launch improvements.

I have been surprised by the number of companies that do not undertake this step. Many do not because the infrastructure has simply gotten so complex that it is a difficult and time-consuming exercise. Not doing it, however, inevitably means ongoing waste. Lacking a map, it is impossible to determine whether new systems or hardware are redundant to or even incompatible with what you may already have. And the longer an organization waits to map its infrastructure, the harder the mapping becomes. Don't put it off.

At the same time, however, don't try to map it all at once. First, prioritize what to map on the basis of importance to the business. If your infrastructure is mainly related to retail point-of-sale, for instance, begin by noting which systems and hardware relate directly to point-of-sale. Document the age of relevant hardware and software. Also specify accessible alternatives for replacement, so that if there is a need to upgrade, you will know where to get the relevant systems and hardware.

Start with the most critical aspects of infrastructure first and move to less critical ones, eventually documenting the entire infrastructure.

Also, map interdependencies between different parts of infrastructure. This takes time, but is necessary to avoid scrapping one system only to find you have, in effect, unintentionally scrapped another one that depended on it. If you understand interconnections, you can make decisions for one system in a way that trickles correctly through other related systems and hardware.

Many companies outsource infrastructure without first mapping their own IT. In so doing, they lose important details, and the agreement with the external partner is overly optimistic about the complexity involved in the process of outsourcing that portion of the division. A map of your company's own IT is a critical tool for checking the reality of an outsourcing proposal.

Subprinciple 2. Maximize Systems' Up-Time

Systems up-time is in many ways the most important metric of infrastructure. (As mentioned earlier, I will explain other metrics associated with this principle at the conclusion of the chapter, as I will with each principle chapter.) Infrastructure should be up and available. If it is not, then productivity declines, and ultimately revenue may be lost. Simply by monitoring up-time, you can begin the process of improving it. It is impossible to establish up-time goals without first establishing what the baseline for the metric is, after all. Metrics can also dispel people's doubts that a system, for instance, is truly reliable.

A classic mistake is to "fix" system and hardware issues without discovering their root causes. Root-cause analysis means understanding whence the error occurred, and so decreasing the chances that it will recur after being "corrected." Here is an example of a seven-step root-cause analysis that has worked well for our clients:

1. *Document the issue as soon as it arises.* This requires some sort of electronic database, perhaps on the company's intranet, that provides an easy way to log issues. Issues should be catalogued and categorized. Is it a systems issue? Is it a hardware issue? Is it an outage, or is the infrastructure doing something different from what is intended? Tailor categories to your company's situation and needs.

2. *Gather data on the issue.* After the issue is catalogued, more data should be gathered on it—enough detail so that others who are not privy to the initial analysis can understand and, where applicable, replicate the issues. All this should be in plain language.

3. *Identify causal relationships associated with the issue.* The different causal relationships should also be documented. This should build on the interdependency map that is part of your infrastructure roadmap. One system's problems will likely affect other interdependent systems. Conversely, issues that seem to arise in one system may actually be caused by another.

4. *Identify effective solutions that prevent recurrence.* Once the issue has been documented, the cause has been determined, and its impact has been traced, it is up to people who know the most about the systems and hardware in question to come up with possible solutions. In turn, they take a proposal to the actual decision makers. A solution proposal should say

   • What a permanent fix would be using the existing systems and hardware
   • Whether the issue that has arisen is grave enough to warrant replacing the systems or hardware
   • The time and dollars required

5. *Implement the solutions.* Once the solution or solutions have been defined, then it or they should be implemented. There

should be a person dedicated to solving the issue, and that person should report regular updates to at least the head of infrastructure if not the CIO or above, depending on the severity and importance of the issue. Throughout the time that the solution is implemented, solid documentation should be kept so that the steps taken can be retraced in the future if necessary.

6. *Conduct postmortems.* Set dates when you will revisit the issue to ensure that it is resolved. Postmortem analyses will help to determine whether the solution is permanent or not. The documentation kept in step 5 should be reviewed in detail during the postmortem.

7. *Finalize and archive documentation.* Once the postmortem has concluded, finalize the documentation and clarify any points that may render it difficult to understand by others who were not party to the solution. It is also important to maintain a library of these solutions as part of a knowledge management program to facilitate the development of comparable solutions in the future. The library format should be such that others can access it when issues arise again with the same systems or hardware. Also, when comparable issues arise in related areas of infrastructure, these documents can provide vital clues on how to resolve them.

A couple of years ago, we worked with the new CIO of a business-process outsourcing client. The perceptions of IT were fairly good, but some business partners believed that systems were not as reliable as they should be. In other words, they were criticizing system up-time. At the conclusion of our assignment with our client, among other recommendations, we suggested that the IT department keep its up-time metrics up to date for all major aspects of infrastructure. Six months later, they determined that the infrastructure was actually far more reliable than previously thought, and tracking it more actively led to further improving an already impressive baseline. Also, by being able to definitively show the business partners that systems were more reliable than they had perceived, IT gained more credibility, and the bond between IT and the business strengthened.

One must bear in mind the up-time that the company needs to have for different aspects of infrastructure. If there are some systems that only need to be available 97 percent of the time, then attempting to make them available 99.999 percent of the time is a waste of time and effort.

Subprinciple 3. Maintain Your Infrastructure

Once the infrastructure is mapped, and major facets of infrastructure have been documented, and once fires are extinguished and systems are up and running at optimal levels, it is important to schedule maintenance for all major facets of infrastructure. Maintenance planning depends on evaluating the following:

- *Age*. How old is each system? Old infrastructure is not necessarily bad, but the older it is, the more likely it is to have issues.

- *Availability of supporting skills*. What skills are available to support each aspect of infrastructure? As infrastructure ages, the skills necessary to support it may age with it, perhaps to the point of extinction. Waiting for that point is highly risky. Better to anticipate it well in advance.

- *Reliability*. Reliability is easiest to evaluate if you have been tracking systems' up-times, as in subprinciple 2. Systems can be ranked on the basis of their availability. Those that are less reliable should be dealt with sooner. Moreover, warning signs need to be heeded before subtle issues become full-blown problems and outages.

- *Alternatives*. Whether key infrastructure is reliable or not, alternatives should be noted as the infrastructure roadmap is developed and maintained. At some point, all systems and hardware reach their breaking point, and continuing to monitor what new solutions are available to replace them will save you time in the crunch. Potential replacements themselves will change as time passes, so it is important to set aside time and resources to investigate new innovations useful to infrastructure. This is not an easy undertaking, and the need to be abreast of new innovations is one reason companies give for outsourcing infrastructure.

- *Interdependency.* Think about the interdependency of infrastructure, as well, within the context of maintenance. Providing fixes to or updates to one part of the infrastructure may lead to the need to do the same to other aspects of infrastructure that are linked. Note these linkages as a matter of maintenance.

- *Cost to replace.* Understanding the cost to replace systems logically happens when you investigate alternatives. You should study replacement costs as you note inter-dependencies, since replacing one system may require replacement of interdependent ones, as well.

- *Risks inherent in keeping systems.* After investigating costs, you may deem some existing systems too expensive to replace. That may well be an appropriate decision, but it is also important to assess the risks of *not* replacing a system. Some of these risks will pop out as you study a system's age, availability of skills to support it, and reliability. There will come a time when the systems may still seem too expensive to replace but the risk is too high not to do so. Have the appropriate information so that the decision can be accurately weighed.

- *Projected timing for retirement or replacement.* This will be covered in more depth in the next subprinciple.

Another important consideration when contemplating the maintenance of one's infrastructure is planning the timing of the maintenance. Since maintenance often requires that systems or hardware be down for a period of time, the IT department must understand when these outages will have the lowest impact on productivity. Obviously, different aspects of infrastructure need to be available at different times, and as discussed earlier, there are varying levels of criticality and timeliness to infrastructure. These factors must be taken into consideration, as well.

Subprinciple 4. Plan Infrastructure Retirement

Your analysis from subprinciple 3 should lead to a retirement plan for each aspect of infrastructure. Because all systems will eventually need to be replaced, a time horizon should be assigned to all of the company's systems and hardware. Some may be noted as immediate, some may be six months or twelve months, or eighteen months; some others may not be for several years. This analysis should then be put on the infrastructure roadmap so that these replacement dates are worked into budgets and planning activities well in advance of the replacement.

Subprinciple 5. Security

Information security has been a topic of consideration for as long as private matters have been documented. As the ability to share critical, private information over vast distances increased, the need to ensure that it would not get into the wrong hands likewise increased in importance. In the first half of the twentieth century, most high-speed international communication was carried out via Morse code. During the two World Wars, it was used as a way for allies to communicate across large distances, but there was always the ability for the enemies to intercept and interpret messages, and therefore new codes and mechanisms were used to ensure that information was transmitted "securely." These were not perfect, of course.

Security is a central concern for companies today. As businesses and individuals are connected to a greater degree than they have ever been, the threat of security breaches have increased exponentially. To make matters worse, the techniques for securing the many types of mobile data have not been fully established.

The potential threats are manifold, including

- Natural disaster
- Network attacks
- Viruses
- Fraud of various kinds
- Competitor espionage
- Portability of data

Security breaches of these kinds and others can lead to public relations issues, customer loss, compliance issues, and ultimately to lost revenues and profits. We will deal with some thoughts on recovering from these issues when we cover disaster recovery and business continuity in the next section.

As Gregor Bailar, former executive vice president and chief information officer of Capital One and former chief information officer of NASDAQ, puts it, "At NASDAQ, the integrity of the information *is* the product. A stock market is defined by the accuracy, timeliness, and reliability of its data, so we placed considerable emphasis on information security and the protection of data assets. At Capital One the company was built on a strategy called the Information-Based Strategy, using advanced analytics to better match financial offerings with customer needs. Clearly, data were critical to the operation of the business, but beyond that, customers expect a bank to protect the privacy of their information, and Capital One maintains high standards to ensure it meets this obligation."

At both companies Bailar and his team endured thousands of attacks every week. Just prior to his arrival at NASDAQ, that entire stock market suffered an outage when a squirrel gnawed through a non-redundant and highly critical cable. Understandably, security breaches by wild animals were not planned for, but it helped instill a culture of "unconditional fault tolerance and business continuity capability," as Bailar puts it. At both NASDAQ and Capital One, he maintained dedicated teams to counter threats from a wide variety of sources and regularly tested the defenses, developing and testing various scenarios and trying to dream up threats before attackers did. In addition, he had extensive procedures, tests, and rehearsals for a variety of environmental and man-made threats to the operation of both companies and the protection of data.

The International Organization for Standardization (ISO) and the International Electrotechnical Commission (IEC) have developed a "code of practice for information security management."[2] In it these organizations recommend three sources of security requirements:

1. The first source is developed assessing risks of the organization, bearing in mind the company's business objectives.

   a. In this way, threats to assets should be identified.

   b. Vulnerabilities and the likelihood of the threats occurring should also be noted.

   c. The potential impact of these threats should also be estimated.

2. The second source that ISO/IEC notes is the legal, statutory, regulatory, and contractual requirements that an organization, its trading partners, contractors, and service providers have to satisfy.

3. The last source is the particular set of principles, objectives, and business requirements for information processing that an organization has developed to support its operations.

It is best that there be a person or a team tasked with security responsibilities. Infrastructure security tends not to be done well as a second job for an individual or a group of individuals. This body should set standards, develop communications and training materials, and remain abreast both of new threats and of new techniques to prevent them. This team should also maintain metrics to gauge how well the organization is doing relative to infrastructure security. (Specific recommendations on metrics to maintain are provided at the conclusion of the chapter.)

It is of the utmost importance that the security standards be understood by everyone in the organization, and that compliance with them be communicated from the top, not just from the part of the IT department where security resides. Training should be provided for all new employees, and this training should be updated from time to time so that all employees are aware of new potential threats and plans to mitigate risks associated with them.

Also note that there are governmental mandates for security. For instance, publicly traded companies must comply with Sarbanes-Oxley legislation such as Statement on Auditing Standards (SAS) 70, which defines the professional standards used by a service auditor to assess the internal controls of a service organization and issue a service auditor's report.

There are also industry-specific standards that one must be mindful of. Retailers who accept credit card payments must comply with payment card industry (PCI) standards for security. Health care companies must be cognizant of the security standards suggested by the Health Insurance Portability and Accountability Act (HIPAA), which regulates the availability and breadth of group health plans and certain individual health insurance policies. There are infrastructure security components to each of these that need to be taken into consideration. Of course, these regulations are ever changing, and new regulations are proposed and passed frequently, so remaining abreast of these changes and contemplating what it means from a security and compliance perspective is important.

This naturally leads to the topic of disaster recovery and business continuity.

Subprinciple 6. Develop and Test Disaster Recovery and Business Continuity Plans

Developing plans for disaster recovery and business continuity is like investing in life insurance. There may be a tendency to underinvest when one feels healthy, only to regret that decision when one is not. To illustrate the importance of developing these plans, an example may be helpful. In five days in June 2001, Tropical Storm Allison dropped over thirty inches of rain on Waco, Texas, flooding much of the relatively flat city. Many businesses that had put their data centers low in buildings or even underground to help cool them lost those centers. A prominent example was Baylor College of Medicine, which in addition to losing ninety thousand research animals and sixty thousand tumor samples lost twenty-five years of research data in the storm. For many, a lifetime's worth of research was gone.[3]

The horror stories from companies that had sustained damage were enough to make one think long and hard about disaster recovery and business continuity. This is often the case with this investment. Time spent on developing processes, preparing people, and investing in tools are all akin to insurance investments. They do not pay off immediately. In fact, one hopes that they will never pay off at all, but they sure are nice if disaster does strike.

Disaster recovery and business continuity are related, but it is useful to define them separately. Disaster can come about from attack by terrorists or hackers. It can also derive from natural disasters such as floods or earthquakes. Disaster recovery is the process by which business resumes after disaster strikes. Business continuity is a more general term to describe the process by which business resumes not only in the case of disaster, but also when there are issues in the supply chain, or if a key leader leaves the company.

The key in developing disaster recovery or business continuity plans is to imagine the different potential scenarios. Scenarios can begin with disasters (natural disaster, death of a c-level executive, fire at the headquarters, and so on) or with other triggers for business continuity problems (the departure of a c-level executive, the dissolution of a key supplier, the obsolescence of a key technology, and so on). Scenarios should be mapped out, and their probability considered. It is not likely that a business in the Midwest would need a plan in case of a hurricane, but it probably does need to think about tornados.

As Gregor Bailar puts it, he did not intend to become an expert on disaster recovery, but for reasons outside of his control, he has had to enact disaster recovery plans through some of the most famous American disasters of the 2000s. He was the CIO at NASDAQ during the terrorist attacks of 9/11. After he joined Capital One in 2002, he had to manage a large team in the Washington, D.C., area through October of that year when a sniper killed ten people in the region. Then in March of 2006, he was actively planning the integration of a New Orleans–based bank called Hibernia Bank when Hurricane Katrina hit. Successfully leading a company through any one of these challenges would offer a claim to fame. Leading multiple companies through all of them is much more remarkable. Bailar has established several principles that have served him well in each of those scenarios.

First, as he puts it, it is important that one has "planned for the worst and [is] prepared for the most common." This means identifying what the most common potential threats might be. Different natural disasters are more likely in different geographical areas; identifying what those are and planning scenarios around them is critical. Recognizing that the threat of terrorism adds a different element to these plans is also critical. At NASDAQ, Bailar prepared for everything from lightning strikes and floods to a potential explosion of the data center.

In selling these plans to the business, Bailar advises that you ensure that the conversation is grounded in business principles.

"Phrase the need in a business framework, and then determine with the business what is acceptable given the different scenarios," he says. You must understand which aspects of the infrastructure are mission critical, and which ones are less so. You also need to identify the potential for lost revenues or unhappy customers should there be a period when some aspect of the infrastructure is down.

Last, note that not all systems and hardware need to be bullet-proof. Not everything needs to be up and available at all times. If a disaster leads to many parts of the infrastructure going down at once, you will need to prioritize.[4]

Again, taking the inventory suggested earlier in this part should help. Which are the mission-critical systems whose shutdown leads to revenue loss? These need to be backed up first. The company should think about investing in redundant data centers in different locations so that all strategic data is backed up and still accessible should disaster strike the company.

You must understand the pressure points between the different aspects of infrastructure. This interconnectivity, and the potential chain reaction that issues in one area can cause in others is often not contemplated to a great enough extent. Critical functions should be called out, the method of keeping them up and running should be documented, and the procedures to do so should be rehearsed. Note, however, that there may be multiple layers of technology and non-technology components that those functions traverse. Without getting to that level of understanding at least as it relates to the most important aspects of the business and IT infrastructure, many unforeseen issues may result.

Another important step is to map out where people will go under this scenario. If the headquarters building burns down, where will they work? Are the remote-access capabilities such that people could work from home for a while? It is of the utmost importance to determine ahead of time who is responsible for declaring a disaster, opening communications channels, and disseminating such information.

CSO *Security and Risk* magazine recommends the following nine steps in developing a business-impact analysis:[5]

1. Develop and practice a contingency plan that includes a succession plan for your CEO.

2. The employees you thought you could count on to lead in an emergency will not always be available. Train backup emergency leaders as well.

3. Determine offsite crisis meeting places and crisis communication plans for top executives. Practice crisis communication with employees, customers, and the outside world.

4. Invest in an alternative means of communication in case the phone networks go down.

5. Make sure that all employees—and executives—are involved in exercises in which they can practice responding to an emergency.

6. Make business continuity exercises realistic enough to tap into employees' emotions so that you can see how they'll react when the situation gets stressful.

7. Form partnerships with local emergency response groups—firefighters, police and EMTs—to establish a good working relationship. Let them become familiar with your company and site.

8. Evaluate your company's performance during each test, and work toward constant improvement. Continuity exercises should reveal weaknesses.

9. Test your continuity plan regularly to reveal and accommodate changes. Technology, personnel, and facilities are in a constant state of flux at any company.

In pitching the disaster recovery or business continuity plan to the business, it is useful to present it in business terms. On December 6, 2004, LaSalle Bank had a major fire on the twenty-ninth and thirtieth floors of its headquarters building in Chicago. Thankfully for them, the bank had a disaster recovery plan that had been tested as recently as August of 2004. There was a calling tree; alternative locations had been chosen for work in the event of a disaster at the building; and when the real disaster struck, the company did not miss a beat. No critical systems were affected, and the bank continued to do business throughout the recovery. As a result, it received a tremendous amount of positive press for its ability to plan, which brought in additional business in the aftermath.[6]

Disaster recovery and business continuity can be developed over a series of small steps, starting with the key business units and working through the company, and working through strategic infrastructure, eventually covering the entire company.

Subprinciple 7. Improve Your Service Desk

Forrester recently polled 2,138 technology users at U.S. companies on their opinions of their company's IT organization and its technologies. While users are generally satisfied with the technologies their company has adopted, such as desktop technology and business applications, many IT organizations needed to work on their help desk support and communication. Just 53 percent of users report being satisfied or very satisfied with their help desk support. This is cause for concern. For one thing, the help desk or service desk is the face of the IT organization, and a lack of credibility there can easily translate into lower faith in the department generally and, potentially, tighter budgets, longer approval cycles, and a reduction in the overall role of IT in driving business change. Help desk organizations must assess their competencies, find areas for potential improvement, and grow.[7]

Companies can take various steps to improve the help desk function:

- Develop a FAQs list and self-help mechanisms for the company.
  - It is critical that it be useable, or upon instituting this, there will be a tendency to continue to call the help desk by default.
- Develop a help desk topic library that is easy to navigate by help desk staff and that can be used as part of self-help for all associates.
- Define the levels of help desk:
  - The first-tier questions are fit for the first person who answers the phone; hopefully many of these can be addressed through the use of the FAQs and the self-help mechanisms.
  - Second tier often includes a call with an expert in the area where there is an issue.
  - Third tier often involves a site visit by an expert to actually physically help with the issue at hand. This is becoming less prominent, however, as more can be done remotely, as help desk people remotely access computers and other aspects of the infrastructure.
- Keep and monitor metrics.
  - It is critically important to understand who is calling on what topic. The "who" should take into consideration title, department, tenure with the company, and frequency of calls.
  - The topic should be broken out as more data is collected, but some easy ones to pre-populate should include all major categories of infrastructure, business and IT processes, and tool-specific questions.

- How long does it take to resolve each issue? Different categories of issues will have different goals for resolution time, but these should be noted, monitored, tracked, and improved upon.
- The IT department should also track which issues are raised most often, and corrective action should be taken to improve those areas that are asked about most frequently.

- Broadcast those metrics.
  - This provides the incentive for continuous improvement, and it provides proof of value to the business and IT users.

- Continue to refine all of the above.
  - FAQs should be added to and modified as certain topics rise or fall in call frequency.
  - Answers should be modified on the basis of user feedback, especially if new solutions are developed.
  - The topics covered by the different tiers of the help desk should be modified to reflect reality.
  - The method to deliver those remedies should also be refined as new solutions become available.
  - Metrics should be added to, subtracted from, and otherwise modified.

Metrics

Unlike the previous principle, people, infrastructure is much more data-centric. Because it is a principle that IT can shape to a greater extent than others, it is incumbent upon the organization therefore to measure its performance and communicate those measurements. Table 3.1 shows metrics that organizations should consider implementing to gauge the performance of infrastructure.

**Table 3.1.   Metrics for Building and Maintaining a Robust IT
Infrastructure.**

Subprinciple	Introductory Metrics	Advanced Metrics
Create an Infrastructure Roadmap	• Percentage of all major systems and hardware mapped with maintenance and retirement schedules included • IT infrastructure spending as percentage of IT spending • IT infrastructure spending as percentage of revenue	• Percentage of new development decisions incorporated into infrastructure roadmap • Percentage of employees aware of infrastructure roadmap
Maximize Systems Up-Time	• Percentage of time systems are online • Percentage of time mission-critical applications are online (higher percentage than the one above) • Number of system down-times	
Maintain Your Infrastructure	• Percentage of all major systems that have maintenance schedules developed • Ratio of scheduled over total down-times	• Number of repeat maintenance requests per problem • Time and dollars spent on maintenance

Table 3.1.   (*Continued*)

Subprinciple	Introductory Metrics	Advanced Metrics
Plan Infrastructure Retirement	• Average systems and hardware age documented for all major systems • Percentage of systems scheduled to retire over period	• Percentage of major systems and hardware with retirement plans • Percentage of systems and hardware to be retired in the three- to five-year time horizon
Security	• Number of information security incidents • Average number of vulnerabilities for system X • Percentage change in number of critical vulnerabilities over X period • Reduce the number of virus infections within the organization by X percent in Y period • Ratio of virus alerts to virus infection	• Percentage of systems compliant with IT security standards • Degree of understanding of security issues among system users • Vulnerability as percentage of total asset value
Develop and Test Disaster Recovery and Business Continuity Plans	• Percentage of mission-critical systems with disaster recovery plans	• Percentage of disaster recovery plans tested

Table 3.1.   Metrics for Building and Maintaining a Robust IT
Infrastructure. (*Continued*)

Subprinciple	Introductory Metrics	Advanced Metrics
Develop and Test Disaster Recovery and Business Continuity Plans, continued	• Percentage of systems and hardware with recovery time objectives (RTO) defined • Percentage of systems with recovery point objectives (RPO) defined	• Percentage of systems and hardware with redundancies • Percentage of systems with RTOs and RPOs met after a disaster
Improve Your Service Desk	• Help desk ticket close rate • Average response time	• Number of issues passed on to higher tiers versus increased first call resolution rate

The Infrastructure Principle and Its Connection to IT's Greater Company Role

Also, unlike almost all of the other principles, the infrastructure principle and the subprinciples associated with it are very much in the IT department's control. Therefore, there is no excuse for the IT department if it does not maintain reliable, accurate, and timely data associated with infrastructure.

Although infrastructure is the most IT-centric of the five principles, the metrics associated with it should be shared with the broader organization. If improvements have been made, this should be celebrated. If metrics have not been met, these should be explained. Failure to achieve infrastructure metrics may uncover weaknesses in the infrastructure, and may provide justification for retirement and replacement of infrastructure, as well.

Principle 3: Manage Projects and Portfolios Effectively

Project and portfolio management offers great opportunity for IT. There is no reason that IT should not be a company leader in this respect. Right now that is not the general case. Excellent management and governance at this level is by no means widespread across IT units. But why shouldn't it be? Consider the high percentage of company budgets that are dedicated to the IT portfolio; that is a good indication that IT organizations have as many if not more opportunities to hone these skills as do other parts of the company.

Of course there are reasons that IT has not been strong at managing projects and portfolios. IT projects were not always given the scrutiny that they should have been. Business executives did not always understand what went into the creation of technology, and therefore were not in a position to push back at the cost and time estimates that were given by their colleagues in the IT department. The need for greater scrutiny is increasing, however, and there are examples of IT departments that have made great strides in improving project and portfolio management.

Testing IT's Mettle

Initially, IT departments typically focused on cost-reduction activities at best, or on "enabling" projects in other departments; what IT did was not perceived, in itself, as enhancing revenue or reducing cost; it stood a degree or two removed from tangible value. From that perspective, it seems clear that a sales division, for instance, needed to be managed and monitored more closely than an IT department: a sales division had an actual, dollar promise on which to deliver, by which it could be judged. But several things have changed this general situation.

First, as technology became pervasive at almost every company, it was difficult to ignore its importance. Savvy competitors began to beat staid, old companies through nimble use of technology. The classic example is Amazon.com versus Barnes & Noble. The former was a creative startup that revolutionized the way in which people thought about shopping for books, and then music, and then everything else. Barnes & Noble, by contrast, had little technical savvy, but it did have comfortable, recognizable bookstores. Barnes & Noble had been around as a printing business since 1873, and as a bookseller since 1917. By dissecting the arcane value chain that governs book publishing and sales, and the fact that 30-plus percent of hardcover adult books are returned through traditional channels,[1] Amazon.com realized that there were ways to apply technology to this not-so-innovative industry and therefore to create new value for itself.

I spent some time at an eCommerce strategy firm in the late 1990s, and I write from experience that every *Fortune* 500 company that we worked with had some fear of being "Amazoned." When the Internet bubble burst in 2000, this took away a lot of this fear, but many success stories like Amazon.com's remained.

A second thing that changed the visibility of IT's management issues was Sarbannes-Oxley (SOX). To quell public concern with the effects of the accounting scandals at companies such as Enron, Tyco International, and WorldCom, the U.S. government enacted this federal law on July 30, 2002. SOX dictated that public companies needed to disclose more about how they spent their money and, in general, it demanded better governance and greater amounts of accountability among executives. This included the IT department, and therefore many companies that had not demanded that the IT department thoughtfully account for every dollar spent suddenly had the government mandate to do so.

A third, broad event was that a greater number of companies from industries that were traditionally thought to be less technology-centric developed significant competitive advantage through creative use of technology. Harrah's Entertainment offers us an example. The gaming industry historically has been thought of as a relationship business. Casino managers and other hosts were encouraged to get to know customers on a personal basis. They collected a vast amount of information on their best customers, but that information largely resided in their minds. If a host moved from one casino to another, he or she took that information with him or her. The value was with the host more than it was with the company.

John Boushy led both marketing and technology when Harrah's would be viewed as a leader in each of those areas. Working with Gary Loveman, a former associate professor of business administration at Harvard Business School who would rise to become chief executive officer of Harrah's, Boushy would establish industry firsts such as the first industry-wide customer database, the creation of the first national loyalty program, and the first yield-management system that provided an expected profitability projections customer by customer. By implementing these systems, the company could systematize what was in the heads of the hosts on the casino floor. In addition, the way in which Harrah's laid out its slot floors and its merchandising decisions were powered by technology. As Boushy puts it, "Technology was viewed as an aid to manage information to create insights that management could act upon." It also knit together departments within the company in a way that was fundamentally new. As Boushy points out, "the fact that information could be accessible so that a financial planning and analysis person could evaluate the effectiveness of a marketing program that was put in place because of feedback that was received by hosts based upon conversations with their guests, and then be able to track the detailed transaction information that Harrah's had about what guests [would do] in the future" led all of those constituents within Harrah's to interact to a greater degree.[2]

As IT departments begin the process of proving their mettle to their companies, it is important that they engage in good governance practices, which ultimately are at the heart of the principle of project and portfolio management. If IT cannot deliver projects on time, on budget, and on scope, then it will not gain the credibility necessary to sit at the strategy-setting table, which is the essence of the principle discussed in the next chapter. This does not sound like such a daunting first step, and yet the statistics are not so good: the Standish Group suggests that only 32 percent of projects are delivered on time, on budget, with required features and functions.[3]

We often describe this principle to clients as the last of three table-setting principles. Together with people, and infrastructure, solid project and portfolio management sets a table for the company to invite IT to more interesting eating—more meaningful things to do on the company's behalf. Business partners within the company who do not have faith in IT's ability to fulfill the first three principles will make sure that the business begins (or continues) to make decisions that have an impact on the IT department without consulting IT's leaders.

For instance, a property and casualty insurance client of ours elected to do a true inventory of all IT projects that were being carried out. The fact that the IT leaders did not have a ready answer to this sort of a question spoke volumes, of course, but what they found was that there was a "shadow IT department" in the form of IT investments made and carried out by IT vendors that the business partners engaged without ever consulting the IT department. There were redundant activities endorsed by different parts of the business. The company invested in competing infrastructures that in some cases made the company less secure and more technically complex.

When business partners were asked why they did this, they simply answered that the IT department could not be counted on to deliver what the business needed.

I have learned not to be surprised by such striking examples of businesses feeling let down by their IT departments. They are all too common. IT absolutely must govern itself in such a way that the rest of the business wants to engage with it in the course of tackling their greatest challenges. After all, the IT department is often the division that suffers most from "hairball" infrastructure that inadvertently arises out of independent decisions, made apart from IT and without a central, governing body.

Over the years, IT executives have been infamously poor at governance based on the classic metrics of being on time, on budget, and on scope. Projects often miss the mark in more than one respect.

Eight Subprinciples of Project and Portfolio Management

Figure 4.1 sequences and summarizes eight subprinciples of project and portfolio management.

Subprinciple 1. Generate Ideas

Idea generation is an obvious place to begin, and there are some simple rules IT leaders can follow to ensure that the best ideas bubble up.

First, consider some common mistakes. For one, often companies allow ideas to be generated and submitted only by senior members of the team. I have never understood the rationale for this. Is there a reason why bright ideas can't occur to a junior member of the staff? In many organizations, strategic planning is a process that is only understood by a select few senior members of the team, which makes it all the more difficult for junior members of the team to contribute ideas that align well to those plans. If

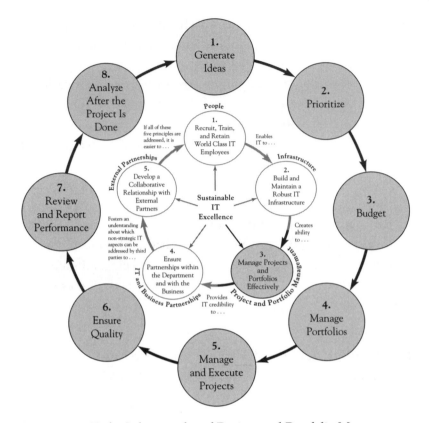

Figure 4.1. Eight Subprinciples of Project and Portfolio Management.

the junior members of the team do not understand which way the ship is pointing, then naturally they may not be positioned well to make suggestions about projects that would best support that vision for the future. Ironically, the junior members of the team are sometimes closest to the issues that need to be resolved. There is tremendous value lost in not asking all members of the team to contribute ideas.

Another common mistake is asking that ideas be submitted only a couple of days per month. A couple of years ago, I worked for a major bank, and the company asked for all new ideas to be submitted one time per year, just prior to budgeting. In some ways, this would appear to make sense: the company knew of all proposed investments, and could calculate how much they would cost, and that would provide a solid, bottom-up view of the budget necessary for the year ahead. The critique of this makes even more sense, however: it is illogical to think that the best ideas occur to people during one period per year. What then if someone has the next blockbuster idea several weeks after the deadline for submitting ideas? The better tactic is to have a rolling idea-submission process.

If the strategic plans of the corporation and business units are made available to a wider swath of people, then the person who originates the idea should first consult the plan to see whether the new idea links well to the plan. Poor linkage should be the first step in filtering out unusable ideas. If it links well, more assessments should be done by a broader range of relevant players in the company. (If it is a technology to be applied to Marketing, then constituents from the IT and Marketing Departments should be engaged.) Ideas should then be submitted upward through a series of higher-authority committees who can assess validity, worthiness of funding, and whether the new ideas should be pursued in the near or long term.

I am suggesting that several committees be established to review new idea submissions on a regular basis. These committees should have a stair-step mechanism whereby ideas are advanced from one to the next based on dollar and time hurdles as a start. More junior people should be empowered to make decisions at the lower committee levels for initiatives that are smaller in terms of finances and duration. Larger initiatives should be passed up to committees with more senior-level participants.

McKesson is the largest health care company in the United States. It has several business units that could each be *Fortune* 500 companies were they independent. As a result the IT department has a great number of initiatives to monitor. In addition, each business unit has its own CIO managing the unique technology needs.

When Randy Spratt, executive vice president, chief information officer, and chief technology officer, became the head of Corporate Information Technology (the centralized IT function), there were two issues that he realized needed to be solved:

- Opaqueness of finances
  - The businesses felt that they had no input or insight into the costs that were being incurred by IT. Therefore, they did not have a way to evaluate it, and therefore there was a natural suspicion that money was not being spent on things that mattered.

- Difficulty aligning the behaviors of IT with the behaviors of business because there was no forum to do it other than through "shuttle diplomacy."
  - People would go from one business to the next and have a series of less-structured conversations, and by the time the last of the eight business units was engaged, the conversations with the first were less relevant.
  - This created a glacial slowness of being able to accomplish change or drive new initiatives that might be supported by IT through the business. That in turn added to the suspicion that corporate IT was unresponsive and slow. The relationship was spiraling down.

Spratt turned Corporate IT into a formal shared service. As he investigated Corporate IT's portfolio of applications and technologies, he identified some that were relevant for only a single business. He pushed responsibility for those to the business as a result. If several business units had applications and technologies that were common but managed separately by each business unit, they were moved into Corporate IT for centralized oversight.

Corporate IT set goals and tracked how well they were being met. Spratt needed to train and hire people to undertake these activities. Likewise, a body of people were needed who could work with the business to develop requirements for the needs that they articulated, and in turn evaluate whether the proposed expenditures effectively meet the requirements.

Spratt coordinated the development of three committees for governance of IT:[4]

1. Governance Board
   - The board is made up of business unit presidents and assorted other executives of the company.
   - It sets policy and budget.
     - Agreement on how much IT will spend year-to-year
     - Development of high-level scorecards with strategic changes that each function would hope to undertake
     - Setting of policy for allocation of funds so that there could be an agreement as to how the business units would divide up funds
   - The board also provides a performance appraisal for Spratt and his group via surveys, a formal process conducted each year.
   - The board was originally set up to govern Corporate IT; its success has led to this being expanded to shared services more generally. The IT shared services was perceived as being a success story in making the group more responsive to the business. In turn, comparable committees were set up for other shared services such as real estate, procurement, and payroll.
2. IT Buyers Council (reports to the Governance Board)
   - The IT Buyers Council is made up of representatives of each of the business units—typically the CIOs—that bring the requirements of that business.
   - It helps determine the technologies that are needed to support the business strategies.

- It sees every major expenditure as a result of the activities that Randy takes on.

  - For example, if McKesson hopes to revamp the network to be responsive to issues related to network robustness, the council would see the plans and the business case and approve them.

  - Corporate IT then would need to be responsive to the needs of the business and bring forward business cases to demonstrate that they can alter their technology infrastructure and landscape to the benefit of the businesses.

- This committee helps McKesson determine how to spend money on the basis of the needs of the businesses.

3. Technology Council (underneath the IT Buyers Council)
   - This council's job is to do the technology evaluations and vendor evaluations.
   - The council stays current regarding the direction in which technology is evolving in order to provide the details to the IT Buyers Council.

     - They evaluate the offerings of various vendors.

     - They remain current on new technologies and solutions that will benefit the company.

Although this structure may not perfectly apply to all businesses, there are some ideas that are almost universal.

- Multiple levels of the business should be engaged, from the most senior people to those who are deeper in the organization.

- They should be engaged together so they understand how their needs and demands compare to those of other parts of the business.

- This provides a wonderful cross-business unit education.
- It also helps take the onus off of IT alone to successfully manage the demand generated from many different parts of the business.

- Each committee should have charters with specific tasks and areas of responsibility.

- If there are multiple committees, then there should be as little overlap as possible between the committees.

- Last, these committees should meet frequently enough to stay relevant, and so the burden of making decisions on the ideas that are submitted can be spread throughout the year rather than doing it only once per year, for instance.

Subprinciple 2. Prioritize

Prioritization is a key function of the review committees I suggested for evaluating new ideas. Criteria must be defined in order to ensure that these committees can effectively prioritize new activities with old ones. Companies that operate without standardized criteria often suffer from ever-changing prioritization. The highest-priority initiatives change too frequently, confusing all participants. As a result, projects tend not to live up to their projections largely because they have not received the focus they deserve. The criteria should help with the process.

On the basis of our work with many World Class IT departments, we at Metis Strategy have seen the following criteria as ones that apply to these companies and those that aspire to join their ranks. They are weighted in descending order:

- Strategic fit
- Cost to benefit analysis
- Project interdependency
- Qualitative benefit versus qualitative change
- Risk analysis

Strategic Fit

Many companies make cost to benefit the primary driver or prioritization. Such analysis matters, but even positive ROI projects should be rejected if they do not support corporate or business unit objectives. That is why we believe strategic fit is the most important criteria. Prioritizing by strategic fit first ensures that the organization maintains a focus on the things that matter most.

Cost-to-Benefit Analysis

We believe cost to benefit analysis is the second-most important criterion. As I noted earlier, IT departments have been given increasing reason to accurately predict project costs; however, benefits projections—whether they be through revenue enhancement or through cost savings—remain highly inaccurate, by and large. This is largely due to the residual effects of the IT department being a division of the company that has not traditionally been thought of as a value generator. Now World Class IT departments make a point of building the necessary estimation skills to accurately predict costs and projected benefits of projects. After the fact, they also evaluate how close the evaluations came. (Post-project analysis will be covered later in this chapter.)

Project Interdependency

Project interdependency—our choice for third-most important criterion—is often simply forgotten. Many projects do not truly operate independently, or at least they should not. It is important to think about how the outputs from one project become inputs for another. Likewise, it is important to understand how investment in any individual project might yield project offspring in the form of new versions of that project. The example we often give for this is an auto company's development of a new sedan that eventually becomes a coupe and then a convertible. These "offspring" may require relatively small new investments (relative to the original) in order to appeal to an entirely new segment of customers.

Conversely, the large investment required for the "parent" project is often daunting, if it is a truly new project. It costs a lot to develop a new facility in which to make an entirely new line of automobile: significant spending on research and development, a long lead time to develop a prototype that is then modified some more, potential retraining for people involved, and so on. The original investment in the "parent" (the sedan) might not have been made without the knowledge that the "offspring" (the coupe and the convertible) would be possible as well.

This is true of all projects. Investing in one project without knowing what other project might be created or affected as a result, whether in the same project family or in another, is operating without full information. Therefore, for each project it is important to evaluate the following:

- Which "predecessor" project, if any, will contribute inputs to the project to be evaluated?
- Which "successor" projects will receive outputs from this project?
- Does this project have the potential for project "offspring"?

Next, these projects should be mapped, perhaps on a flow chart (see Figure 4.2 for an example). Such a map should document interconnections. The timing to commence a given project should depend on what the mapping reveals. When we conduct this analysis with our clients, there are always several "successor" projects that are scheduled to be completed prior to "predecessor" projects. Mapping out this analysis helps to ensure that the order is correct.

Project interdependency analysis is also important because it ensures that decisions are not made in a vacuum. If a project is delayed or canceled, it is important to understand whether these modifications to the original plan will have an impact on other project investments.

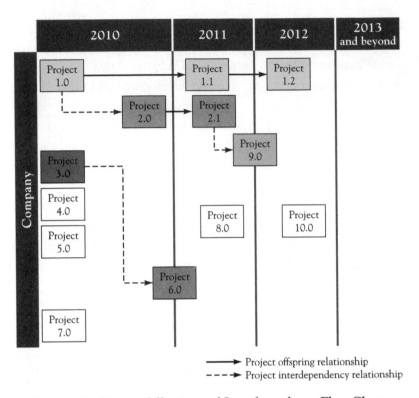

Figure 4.2. Project Offspring and Interdependency Flow Chart.

This analysis also provides an advantage to those projects that are "enabler" projects, meaning those that do not generate value on their own but beget value through facilitating the creation of other projects. If a project is truly the most important project in the portfolio, and it is dependent on another project for critical inputs, then the preceding project is also important. This should count for something when prioritizing projects within a given portfolio.

Qualitative Benefit versus Qualitative Change

We regard the analyses of qualitative benefit and qualitative change together as fourth-most important. The qualitative benefit analysis evaluates the degree to which projects benefit the customer versus the company (Figure 4.3). Projects can focus on both, one, or

Benefit Matrix

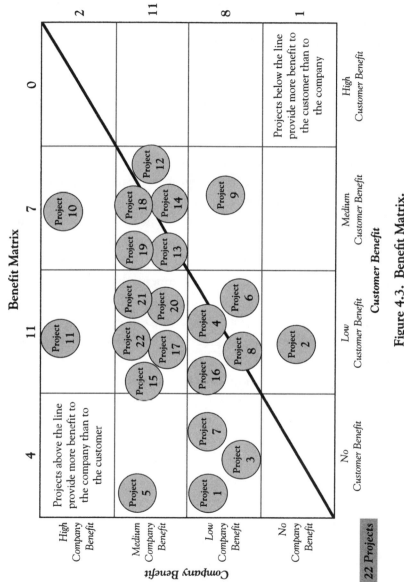

Figure 4.3. Benefit Matrix.

neither. (An example of a project that benefits neither but still would be prioritized highly might be one that responds to a government regulation. The Year 2000 projects that most major corporations invested in heavily was such a project.) At the corporate level over the long term, there should be a balance between customer and company benefit. For short periods, there may be reason for an imbalance, say the need to develop new internal processes in order to innovate over the long term, or the need to focus on the customer due to low customer satisfaction numbers. Being imbalanced over the long term can be perilous, however. Long-term focus on customer-centric investments without corresponding internal process renewal may mean that competitors cannot innovate from a process perspective. General Electric has been able to successfully strike this balance by institutionalizing many process innovations, and by implementing the Six Sigma program. Focusing on internal processes without corresponding investments in customer-centric investments, however, may make it easy for the competition to out-market the company.

The qualitative change analysis distinguishes between changes in technology and changes in process (Figure 4.4). High degrees of technology change without corresponding process change can be dangerous, as instituting radically new technology should involve the implementation of new processes. Again, there should be a balance over the long term between the creation of new processes and the addition of new technologies. It should be noted, however, that the company should not focus only on creating new technologies and processes; it should also focus on leveraging those that are already in place. This represents harvesting the "low-hanging fruit." Therefore, it is important that there be a balance between the new creation, and leveraging existing processes and technologies.

Once these two analyses are conducted, then they should be compared. Portfolios of projects that have a lot of process and technology change without much corresponding benefit to clients or the company are unduly risky. Again, a balance should be struck.

Change Matrix

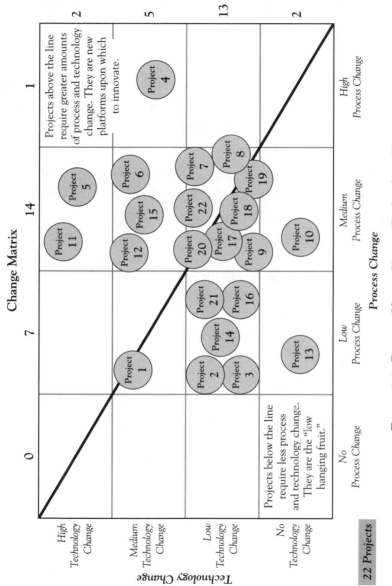

Figure 4.4. Process Change Versus Technology Change.

There may be other criteria to add, of course, including important industry- or company-specific ones. The same criteria should be applied to all projects, so that "apples" can be compared with "apples."

Risk Analysis

The fifth and last criterion that we believe should be used to evaluate projects and portfolios is risk. We traditionally evaluate risk along the lines of five categories:

- *Technology risk.* Technology risk is the degree to which the technology that will be included as part of the project (whether developed from scratch or purchased from a vendor) is new to the company or industry, for instance. The newer and less tested the technology, the greater the risk. Also, projects that use technology that does not fit well with the company's existing infrastructure are also risky. These are not in and of themselves reasons to cancel projects, but identifying that projects have these risks is reason to ask additional questions and potentially to proceed with caution.

- *Management risk.* This refers to the degree to which a project will be easy or difficult to manage. If, for instance, a project will involve hundreds of people across multiple countries, then it is safe to say that there is a significant degree of management risk. It is therefore important to develop processes to mitigate this risk.

- *Implementation risk.* Implementation risk is determined by factors such as whether the project will take many months or years to implement, and whether the benefits will likewise take a long time to realize. The longer the lag time between project commencement and conclusion and benefit realization (which often do not begin until project implementation) the greater the risk. For these projects, it is often beneficial to pilot the project or to develop a prototype in order to more quickly test the validity of the project. Innovative companies are always willing to "fail fast" and shut down projects that prove not to be as successful as they were thought to be, but it requires a well-thought-out project-incubation process to do so effectively.

- *Financial risk.* Financial risk concerns whether a given project has the potential to expose the company to losses if it is unsuccessful. In recent years, many retailers have undergone major replacements to their point-of-sale solutions. In several cases, these have involved replacing home-grown systems that had been "duct-taped" together over many years with external systems run by companies who specialize in point-of-sale solutions. As the name suggests, point-of-sale systems operate precisely at the point where revenues happen for companies, and if these projects are not undertaken successfully, this can lead directly to lost revenues.

- *External risk.* External risks include those associated with
  - Economic changes
  - Changes in regulations that affect the company
  - The potential for increased litigation toward the company
  - Changes in the competitive landscape or aggressive moves by competitors

It is important to evaluate how these and similar potential actions or changes could affect the success of a given project.

High risk does not necessarily make a project bad. As with investments in one's personal investment portfolio, often one must accept some risk in order to achieve higher returns on those investments. The same principle applies to project investments.

As with one's personal portfolio, there should be varying degrees of risk across the investments—some high, some low. A low-risk portfolio itself is risky, as it suggests low levels of creativity and potential for innovation.

Develop contingency plans. Often the person or people who have developed a project idea are so taken with the idea that they conclude that it is the only way in which to accomplish the strategy behind the project. This is a great folly. In the next chapter, we will go through the necessity of creating strategic plans that are divorced of project language, and tying projects to those plans only after they (the strategic plans) have been created, but it is worth noting while covering the topic of project risk that choosing one solution without contemplating other potential options is itself risky.

If a project relies heavily on a single vendor or a single vendor product, for instance, the demise of that vendor could be very risky. Developing contingency plans serves two purposes:

- If the chosen path leads to failure, there is a backup plan to which the company can turn in order to accomplish the underlying strategy.

- By forcing the conversation regarding contingency plans, one may determine that the contingency plan is actually the best option to pursue, and the original plan will then become the contingency plan.

There are certainly other risk categories that may be used. A pharmaceutical client of ours suggested that we add strategic risk. A financial services client of ours suggested adding human resources risk. There may be other categories to add that are even more tailored to a company or an industry. The point, however is that risk needs to be quantified and weighed. Mitigating risks through the creation of contingency plans is necessary.

With strong criteria like the ones just described, prioritization becomes both easier and more objective.

Subprinciple 3. Budget

Once projects are prioritized, the IT department can budget with greater confidence. Companies often budget from the top down. For example, say the IT budget was $100 million last year, and revenue projections for the year ahead are up 5 percent, so as a result, the IT budget can increase 5 percent as well. Therefore the budget for the year ahead is $105 million. There is nothing wrong with applying this sort of logic, but it is important to complement this perspective with a bottom-up view of what the company will get for a hefty investment. After all, any given year may produce a particularly high-value crop of potential projects. If that is the case, a higher spend may be justified.

Prioritizing first makes the budgeting process easier. The prioritization should yield a list from first to last among the projects proposed, and the top-down budget number should allow a first line to be drawn somewhere down the list. If the proposed projects total $125 million in potential spending, and the top-down budget is $105 million, then the line should be drawn after the project that is within the $105 million cap. This should not conclude the budget exercise, however. The company should then evaluate the potential benefits to be garnered from additional investments.

If this is an exercise that is conducted for IT projects related to each of the business units, then this should be a separate exercise for each of the business units, and at the corporate level. The bottom-up perspective should help to determine whether the company should take dollars from one business unit and provide them to another on the basis of the projected value of investments. Of course, understanding that this "horse-trading" exercise is a possibility provides a strong incentive for those providing the project assessments to perform accurate benefit estimations.

Since best practice is to allow ideas to emerge organically and year round, it is important that budgets include placeholder amounts for projects that will inevitably come up mid-year. The best project idea for the year may arise after the budget is locked in. If there is no wiggle room for such projects, they won't happen or won't succeed. As a rule of thumb, we have often seen 5 to 10 percent of a budget recommended as a reserve for these mid-year projects, but you should determine a more accurate figure by tracking your actual percentage over the course of three to five years. It may be higher or lower.

Subprinciple 4. Manage Portfolios

Once the portfolio is prioritized, and the budget is locked in, it is necessary to manage the portfolio. I believe most major companies believe they do portfolio management, but a surprising number do not do it well. True portfolio management should involve the following:

- Meetings at regular intervals to discuss the health of the portfolio
- A program management office to monitor all projects on a regular basis
- Tools to help gather information from project managers so that senior team members can be notified as soon as issues arise and take action
  - These should include dashboards that collect uniform data from across projects.
- Delay or cancellation of projects due to nonperformance
  - Performance should be monitored relative to on-time, on-budget, and on-scope metrics at a minimum.
- Redistribution of people and funds as projects are completed, delayed, or canceled

This list is not exhaustive, but does cover some of the most important attributes of portfolio management. Among the many

IT departments with which we have had the pleasure of working, even some of the best do not do them all.

Meetings should be held at regular intervals because absent any major event, like a certain project going well beyond projected budget, there should be time-based reviews to monitor some of the less obvious changes that should be examined more closely. Wherever possible, people who are responsible for projects should present information about them and provide details on progress made, goals not accomplished, and impediments to meeting upcoming milestones. This information can be presented in person, by phone, or electronically. The simple process of having these regular updates ensures that people do not shirk their duties and attempt to operate under the radar, so to speak.

Although some companies continue to find the concept controversial, it is a good idea to institute a program management office (PMO) within the IT department. This is now essentially a given among World Class IT departments. PMOs are run by people who do not have a stake in any of the projects, but rather monitor the milestones associated with each project to ensure that the project is operating as expected, and, where it is not, to take appropriate action. The PMO should help identify needs that emerge in the IT portfolio directed toward one business unit that are similar to those of a portfolio directed toward another business unit, and ensure that redundant investments are not made.

The larger a company becomes the more important it is that it institute tools to facilitate portfolio management. *Fortune* 500 IT departments often have hundreds of projects going on at any given time, and they may be run around the world. Having one repository for all of the important data on these projects is important.

Note that such databases are only as valuable as the least accurate piece of data in them. If data do not remain up to date for any project, it calls into question the quality of the data for all projects. Therefore, it is critically important to ensure that project managers who contribute the regular updates on projects do so in a timely basis.

The dashboards for each project should include the data I mentioned earlier under subprinciple 2, Prioritize. Of course, it should also include the staffing demand and supply for each, timing for each, and information on relevant milestones. In addition, issues should be gathered and tracked to resolution. If, for instance, a project manager is needed for the project, and none is currently available, that needs to be called out so that higher authorities will be alerted to the issue and take appropriate action. Figure 4.5 shows a sample dashboard.

One key portfolio management problem is an inability to cancel projects. Nearly 80 percent of the companies with which we have worked have indicated that they do not cancel projects once they have commenced. This is antithetical to a healthy innovation process in which companies should experiment with new ideas, knowing full well that some will be canceled once a prototype is available and tested. All too often, sunk cost is the justification for project continuation. "We have already spent many millions of dollars on the project, so we can't possibly cancel it," executives argue. This is simply foolish.

This sends out the wrong signals to those who run projects, as well. It stands to reason that one will not be held accountable for budget overruns if projects are never canceled because of them, for example. World Class IT departments are comfortable delaying or canceling projects if the hypotheses and assumptions on which the project approval was based turn out to be flawed. Developing this discipline is critically important to ensure that portfolio management is done correctly, not to mention that it is a way for the IT department to demonstrate that it is a responsible steward of the corporation's money.

If the company has prioritized its activities effectively, then if a project is placed on hold or canceled, the next project on the list should enter the hopper, assuming the resources in people and dollars fit.

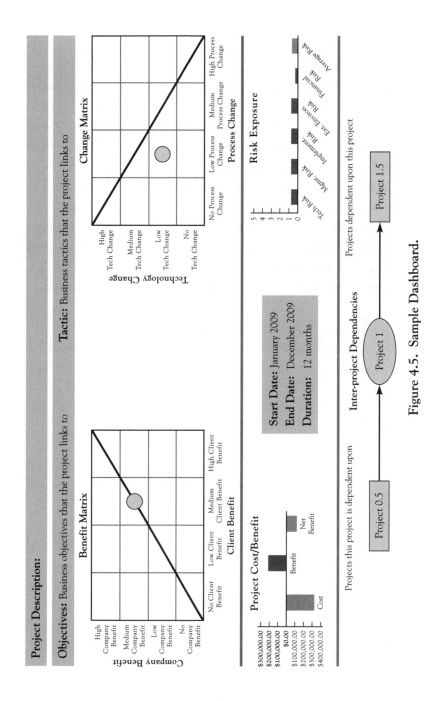

Figure 4.5. Sample Dashboard.

Subprinciple 5. Manage and Execute Projects

As I noted earlier, project management and execution are areas where IT leaders should be well positioned to lead the corporation, because the IT department typically develops and leads as many projects as (if not more than) any other part of the company. Success in this area depends on a repeatable methodology. World Class IT departments have a well-documented project management methodology, and a version of it is used for all projects. I say *version* because the methodology should be thought of as a toolkit rather than as a recipe. *Recipe* tends to imply that each step can and should be followed precisely. The project management methodology should be like a toolkit, in effect, of hammers, screwdrivers, wrenches, and pliers. Some jobs require them all, others only one, but the entire toolkit is always available and kept in mind.

This is often the biggest hurdle in institutionalizing a project management methodology. People complain that it slows them down, as there are new steps to contemplate, new templates to use, and new reviews to conduct as a result. Some of this is due to the natural tendency for a process to need to take a while in order to do the following:

- Analysis
  - Business idea generation
- Concept development
  - Business analysis
- Planning
  - Development proposal, including a project plan, resource determination, and a decision checkpoint
- Development
  - Requirement analysis
  - Solutions design

- Coding
- Testing
- Rollout
  - Production deployment
  - Infrastructure management
  - Documentation
  - Support

Given the preponderance of vendors that now make up IT staff, some of whom take over major portions of the IT function, it is important to ensure that vendors comply with the methodology as well. Metis Strategy has worked with a great number of companies that have undergone major outsourcing, and my colleagues and I have found that the failure to align project management methodologies and language can be a real hindrance to these relationships. If a vendor has a better-thought-out methodology than that of the IT department with which it is engaged, it may be best to follow the vendor's method.

World Class IT departments recognize that project management skills are not easy to garner. Many companies view project managers as people who hold the list of activities that must be accomplished during the life of a project and then check off the items as they are accomplished. This passive role is not true project management at all. Project managers should be more familiar with the details of a project than anyone else. They should lead the team that is charged with developing the project. When milestones are not met, they should be held accountable. If projects meet all of the key metrics associated with them, the manager should be rewarded.

- IT leaders must find creative ways to identify true project management talent.
- Enforce the use of one project management tool and method to be used across the IT department.

- Develop detailed matrices detailing new responsibilities of different people and skill types under the new PM model.
- Develop true go or no-go stage gate evaluations.

Subprinciple 6. Ensure Quality

Quality assurance (QA) is a step in the development lifecycle that is often inadequately addressed, if it is addressed at all, because it takes up valuable time, and if it is done correctly, it costs money. It is invaluable, however, because if QA is done correctly it can ensure that the technology that the department releases is high quality and will not require constant fixes after its release.

There are many guiding ideas to QA, and some may be unique to a given company, but from my experience, the following are nearly universal:

- *Formalize test plans*. Up-front, formal test planning enables both the QA and Development teams to know what to test, when to test it, and how long testing will take. An application's test plan document includes the application test strategy, test requirements, time estimates, identification of resources, and a project test schedule. Once test plans are in place, all project stakeholders, including Development, should review test planning documents for completeness.
- *Clearly define QA processes and quality gates*. A good QA process defines the entry and exit criteria for the hand-off of code between Development, the QA group, and Production. It is a documented process, agreed upon by all stakeholders, and coordinates individuals' work on common projects. A formal QA process reduces the risk of missed deadlines or entering production with open performance and functionality issues.

- *Involve QA early in the development lifecycle.* The QA and Development groups need to work together from the project's inception. The QA lifecycle should parallel the development lifecycle to maximize the probability of eliminating application defects early in the lifecycle. Inclusion of QA at every stage of development reduces the number of architectural and design defects delivered into production and lowers the risk of costly application rework.

- *Document requirements.* Documented application requirements are the yardstick by which everything is measured throughout the software development lifecycle. Development must work closely with the business and application owners and the QA group early in the lifecycle of the project to create a set of testable, documented requirements and have processes and tools in place to manage any changes to requirements. Test cases should be traceable to directly reflect requirements.

- *Use a centralized test group separate from development.* A QA group distinct from Development should perform testing. The central QA group creates standards for testing, maintains those standards for all development projects, and oversees integrated functional and performance testing for all applications. The cost of duplicate hardware and software is reduced and QA knowledge, responsibilities, and best practices are centralized.

- *Allocate adequate time for test execution.* The QA group should have adequate time to perform full system testing and oversee user acceptance testing before the application is released into production. Proper planning will allocate sufficient test execution time and accommodate development delays and fixed date-driven go-live schedules.

- *Represent production in a stable test environment.* Real-world application usage should be tested in a lab containing test equipment that represents the application production environments. Test environments should include a test database that can be restored to a known constant for consistency in repeating the test cases as the application changes. Staff and lab resources should be managed through a master schedule for testing with the QA environments.

- *Ensure that the QA organization is adequately prepared to use and support test automation tools.* QA organizations should focus on efficient test case design, automated processes, and automated test script maintenance. Test automation requires new technology training, new processes, and organizational change. Tool-specific training and mentoring should be provided to employees. Rather than use record-playback techniques, modular, data-driven test automation processes should be developed. People-intensive manual test execution should be reviewed and managed for automation opportunities.

- *Institute defect tracking processes and tools.* Defects should be tracked formally at each project phase so they can be traced through their correction or removal early before entering production. Defect reports that link to specific test cases and requirements streamline remediation and, with proper metrics and baselines, can assist in application readiness decisions.

Subprinciple 7. Review and Report Performance

Earlier I mentioned the need to review portfolios on a regular basis. Conversely, each project must provide these updates so that the portfolio reviews are accurate. Portfolio performance reporting is challenging because different projects have different numbers of milestones, and each may be at a different stage of the project lifecycle. The portfolio reviews can't happen each time an individual project reaches a milestone. Rather these projects must be viewed all at the same time. Therefore, performance reporting must be both milestone and time driven. As milestones are reached, and stage gates of the lifecycle passed, then this should trigger the need to report what has been accomplished or not as the case may be. Likewise, if the portfolio reviews happen monthly, then even if no milestone has been reached and no stage gate has been passed, an update should be provided, even if there is not much new information to provide. It bears repeating that reports are only as good as the least accurate information provided.

Another separator of merely great IT departments from World Class ones is the tracking of benefits. Typically, benefits from projects, be they in the form of added efficiency, general cost cutting, or revenue enhancement, do not become clear until after the project is completed. In fact, often it is months and at times even years before full benefits are achieved. Therefore, it takes discipline to continue to monitor projects that were completed many months prior, at least from a new development perspective. It is important to do so, however as this is the ultimate score to keep: is the IT department delivering on the value it has promised? If it is not, questions should be asked to determine the reason. Of course, if it is, that should be pointed out, as the IT department should continually look for opportunities to burnish its credentials. As it becomes more like other business divisions, it should think about value creation and value monitoring in a similar fashion.

Subprinciple 8. Analyze After the Project Is Done

Much like quality assurance and performance tracking, post-project analysis is often skipped or done hastily. This neglect is intrinsically linked with performance monitoring, since, as mentioned in the prior section, benefits are typically realized after the project has concluded. Of course, it is not until the project is completed that the cost side and the processes that guided the project also can be truly evaluated. World Class IT departments do not lose the opportunity to take advantage of the learning loop that post-project analysis provides. If estimates were off on time, dollars, or scope, this is the time to investigate the reasons.

Post-project analysis is a key step in honing the organization's estimation skills. When future projects arise that are similar to these projects, it is critical that the same mistakes not be made again. If a member of the IT team can say, "this project is quite similar to a project we undertook a couple of years back, and we were off in our estimates due to the following reasons . . . " the team can ensure that the estimates will be that much more precise the second time around.

Metrics

Project management, portfolio management, governance; these are areas in which IT should become "best in class" for the company. The reason is that IT departments tend to have so many and in some cases the majority of projects for a company as the percentage of project costs dedicated to IT projects increases. The proof of this is in the metrics (Table 4.1). I have listed a great number of metrics here. I must reiterate that the point is not to institute all of these. If an IT department attempted to do so, it probably would be keeping too much data, which can be almost as problematic as keeping too little data. Rather, I have included so many ideas so that the reader can have many options to choose from.

Effective IT Project and Portfolio Management and IT's Wider Company Influence

Again, if the IT department is to become the leader of the company in the topics of this chapter, as I contend should be the goal, then the metrics are the proof. The organization should set its sights high in this area, and it should broadcast its successes and failures to the business to provide the right incentives for IT to continue to improve.

Table 4.1.   Metrics for Managing Projects and Processes Effectively.

Subprinciple	Introductory Metrics	Advanced Metrics
Generate Ideas	• Number of new ideas (projects) submitted or logged in during X period • Percentage of budget spent on new ideas (projects) • Percentage of logged ideas being investigated or pursued by the company (in the pipeline) • Number or percentage of employees involved in idea generation • Number of hours (or percentage) each employee spends on idea generation	• Percentage of all IT initiatives with new benefits to customers or the company • Average time from idea log to business case development (approval, kick-off, and so on) • Average time from idea log to fully functional product • Number of new ideas (projects) submitted or logged during X period as percentage of projects approved or initiated • Ratio of IT budget spent on new ideas versus existing programs and "keeping the lights on" • Percentage of ideas logged in during X period aligned with strategic objectives
Prioritize	• Percentage of IT spending on strategic objectives	• Percentage of projects cancelled or put on hold after approval or kick-off relative to all projects

Table 4.1.   Metrics for Managing Projects and Processes Effectively.
(Continued)

Subprinciple	Introductory Metrics	Advanced Metrics
Prioritize, cont'd.	• Number of prioritized initiatives relative to other initiatives (percentage or ratio) • Number of times the portfolio is reviewed and prioritized over a period • Number of approval steps or meetings to establish, confirm, or revise prioritization	• Percentage of resources dedicated to prioritized initiatives versus other initiatives during fiscal period • Percentage change of projects' rank from development onward • Average percentile prioritization change upon review
Budget	• Ratio of actual approved IT budget to requested budget during last decision-making period • Percentage of IT projects budgeted to track during X period • IT budget as percentage of total budget • IT budget per number of employees	• Percentage or reserve funds relative to total IT budget • Percentage of IT expenditures delivering new functionality

Table 4.1.   (Continued)

Subprinciple	Introductory Metrics	Advanced Metrics
Manage Portfolios	• Number or percentage of initiatives in different strategic areas and nonstrategic areas • Average project risk and portfolio risk	
Manage and Execute Projects	• Percentage of ongoing projects on time, on budget, on scope during current last period • Percentage of completed projects on time, on budget, on scope during current last period • Percentage of projects led by nonproject managers • Number of issues discovered during project lifecycle • Percentage of projects accepted without further change at the initial completion of the project • Percentage of projects with total cost of ownership calculated	• Average cost, budget, overrun • Number of change requests as percentage of requirements or functionalities • Number of projects (or percentage of total) in each stage of the project lifecycle • Project manager to staff ratio • Number of projects per project manager

Table 4.1.   Metrics for Managing Projects and Processes Effectively.
(Continued)

Subprinciple	Introductory Metrics	Advanced Metrics
Ensure Quality	• Number of severe defects as percentage of requirements or functionalities • Change in defect fix times over X period • Average cost of fix or change • Average resolution time of bugs or defects	• Percentage of reusable components • Percentage of work (days, FTEs) spent on maintenance tasks • Cost of quality— training review or inspection, rework or retest—as percentage of total project effort • Level of compliance with standards, frameworks, and so on
Review and Report Performance	• Percentage of projects past deadlines, over budget, or out of scope where corrective action has been taken • Percentage of projects that regularly report performance • Average time, budget, scope overrun in X period	• Rate of delivery of units of work (lines of code, function points, and so on) • Average time on defect repair, by type of defect • Value derived from reuse (days saved, dollars saved) • Hand-offs between internal organizations • IT performance against service-level agreements

Table 4.1.   (Continued)

Subprinciple	Introductory Metrics	Advanced Metrics
Analyze After the Project Is Done	• Percentage of projects with customer or user evaluation of IT products • Percentage of projects realizing projected benefits • Number of adjustment and changes made for future projects	• Average end-user satisfaction score • Percentage of deviations from initial requirements and project management doc (scope, money, time) • Number of spin-offs (project offspring) • Percent of deliverables completed within plus or minus 10 percent of estimate

The IT departments are so good at project management, portfolio management, and governance in general, that they "export" their talent to the rest of the organization so that others can learn from IT. This not only has the benefit of improving these capabilities company-wide, it leads to greater cross-pollination in general between the IT department and the company at large. This can lead to better relations between IT and the business, better idea generation, and even better standardization of processes. The latter can lead to greater efficiencies, and better throughput of non-IT projects, as well.

Project management, portfolio management, and governance cannot be done in a vacuum. Projects that are undertaken on behalf of the business should engage the business, and therefore the metrics associated with project and portfolio success should be agreed to by the business, and the business should be encouraged to take ownership, as well. One of the reasons that IT projects are often delayed is due to changing business requirements. Ensuring that the business understands the potential time and cost implications to changing requirements after the project has commenced is important.

Principle 4: Ensure Partnerships within the IT Department and with the Business

Business alignment has for some time been described as the "holy grail" for IT departments. Being truly aligned with the business suggests that the IT department understands the needs of the business, helps shape the plans that the business develops, and is viewed as a true partner to the business. This is a legitimate goal for every IT department.

Why Wasn't Alignment Principle 1?

As I have introduced the ideas described in this book at a wide range of companies, several of our CIO clients have asked why business alignment is not the first principle represented. Their logic continues, "If the ultimate determinant of value for IT is value delivered to the business, then shouldn't this come first?" They have a point. In fact, no matter the state of the IT department, I have advised CIOs who are new to their current position that although they should begin by interviewing members of their own team to understand the strengths and weaknesses of the department, they also should spend at least as much time with the business. This should include not only the senior members of the business units but also people deeper in the organization. It is important to get their perspectives on the strengths and weaknesses as well, of course, but the simple act of asking questions demonstrates that new efforts will be made to ensure that the IT department achieves business alignment.

Yet it is critical that the building blocks of the first three principles be in place in order to truly achieve business alignment. Beginning the dialogues is the first step. Ensuring that the IT department can right past wrongs and improve performance is another item altogether. If the IT department is not populated with business-savvy employees who can translate business needs into IT solutions, then it will have a credibility problem, and business alignment will be difficult. If IT infrastructure is not reliable, and a greater amount of time than is necessary is spent fighting the fires started by the lack of reliability, then IT leaders will have less attention to pay to the needs of the business, and this will impede progress toward business alignment. If the IT department does not have a solid governance process in place along with a well-thought-out project and portfolio management process, then it will not be able to deliver projects in a timely manner, and the business may elect to partner with IT vendors rather than the internal IT department. This is why the first three principles are key building blocks to ensure that principle 4 is possible.

Across many industries and geographies, companies continue to think of the IT department as a support organization. Almost by definition, this means that the business and the IT department are not aligned. They have not forged a partnership. This is a shame, and IT leaders have a significant role to play in changing it. Whenever I hear CIOs say they wish they were viewed more strategically, but that they have not gained the invitation, I inwardly question their true leadership abilities. If you know the current situation is untenable, then do something about it! In many ways, the first three principles, if enacted properly, offer a path toward engaging the business in a new way. The IT department must prove its value by doing the little things well. Hiring and keeping the best people, managing the infrastructure such that it is available nearly 100 percent of the time, and delivering projects on time, on budget, and on scope are each easier said than done, but if one carves each of these principles into the logical substeps suggested by the subprinciples, then it is not so daunting. Moreover, by instituting metrics that demonstrate to the business that progress has been made, it will be that much clearer that the IT department deserves to be considered a true partner of the business.

The CIO alone cannot forge a true partnering relationship with the business for his or her department, however. It also requires a new breed of IT associate. I have mentioned several times that IT departments suffer from the traditional differences between themselves and the business. These differences include education, training, language, interests, and so on. The IT associate of the future needs to know technology but also needs to have a healthy interest and curiosity about the business. Many CIOs in the past did not do a good enough job of ensuring that their employees were educated on what the business does.

I often recommend that IT executives adorn the IT department with evidence of the business that the IT department is a part of. I recently worked for an IT department for a major retailer, and whenever I met with executives in Marketing or in the Services divisions of the company, for instance, I would see hot new products that the company sold, and there would be evidence of how the Services arm helped customers use those products. When I would return to the IT department, it could have been the IT department of a manufacturer, or of a health care company. There was not a shred of evidence of the field the company operated in. If IT employees are to be innovative in their thinking, it is important that everyone be reminded where the company earns its revenues, and to provide the impetus for everyone to think about where the path to innovation lies.

Under principle 1 ("people"), I mentioned that the best companies develop rotation programs in which associates flow in between the business and IT. Each time this is done, a new bridge is built between what are traditionally islands of the corporation. This is such an important exercise that it bears returning to this topic again in light of the development of partnerships between the business and the IT department. There is no better way to align than to walk a mile in your partner's shoes. Rotational programs allow for a true understanding of how different parts of the company work, how they differ, how they react to change, how ideas are generated and vetted. It also reduces the barriers based on language and experience.

Although it is a nascent trend, the reverse is also happening, not only at the more junior levels, but even for the top position. More and more CIOs are emerging from the business, or at least these CIOs have spent some time in their formative years professionally in business roles before ascending to the highest post in IT. This is a shrewd move both for the company and for the CIO who navigated that path, as it is not natural to all CIOs to understand the business, to anticipate its needs, and to suggest solutions to the business before the business itself has anticipated those needs fully.

This trend will continue for many years to come however because members of Generation Y and to a great extent Generation X have an innate understanding and interest in technology, having been introduced to it at such an early age. I recall marveling as a child that my father spent most of his youth without a television. People born in the 1980s and to a greater extent the 1990s and 2000s will marvel that we who were born prior to those decades operated without computers and the Internet through our formative years. I am constantly reminded of this as I speak with young associates in my firm. Many of them majored in business and liberal arts disciplines, and never took a single engineering or computer science course, and yet they have an innate understanding of technology. They are never intimidated by technology. As a result, I think it will be much easier for people with those same business and liberal arts majors who take jobs in marketing, sales, or finance, to name three common business tracks, and who hold the title of CIO as their first "C-level" experience.

IT departments should find those "digital natives" in the business who have been steeped in the disciplines of the business units where they have worked, but who have a strong aptitude and curiosity about technology. This cross-pollination is certainly a win-win for IT and the business.

Sheleen Quish: One Great Example

Although Sheleen Quish is of neither Generation X or Generation Y, she was well ahead of her time in understanding that the IT department offered a unique perch within the corporate structure because of its relationship with all parts of the business. She had no formal technology-centric training, and she had spent her entire career on the business side in marketing and operations roles. In 1993, she was given the opportunity to run IT at Blue Cross and Blue Shield of Kentucky. Quish succeeded because she had built up a great deal of trust and respect while she ran different parts of the business. Therefore, as she made the transition into IT, business alignment increased almost immediately because she understood as a former user of IT how the business could use IT's services, as well as where she had been pleased or let down by the department previously. Also, as an outsider, she was able to ask the "ignorant" question, forcing people to defend what may have been faulty or at least flawed logic behind what was deemed to be conventional wisdom. She embraced this outsider's status, but also embraced the people who populated her new department.

Quish has subsequently led IT departments at the Signature Group, Unitrin, U.S. Can, and Ameristar, where she is currently the CIO. In between these stints, she has also done IT consulting, and she has been a member of the editorial board of *CIO* magazine. To have meaningful stints at such a wide array of organizations in a variety of industries, and to do so in an area in which she had no formal training proves that with a solid understanding of how business needs can be met with technical solutions, a curiosity to explore areas in which one is not expert, and a willingness to ask questions and even to ask for help when necessary, business leaders can become technology leaders.

Businesses are savvy to find business leaders like Quish who can bring a business sensibility to IT, since, as I argue throughout the book, the best IT departments are run like businesses. This is a key way in which alignment can be achieved.

Five Subprinciples of Partnership within IT and with the Business

For IT executives who hope to climb the rungs toward World Class IT performance relative to IT and business partnerships, there is, again, a path to follow, shown in Figure 5.1.

Subprinciple 1. Communicate Well with the Business

Communication is the most important building block in constructing bridges between the business and the IT department. So many of the traditional issues between these peer organizations result from poor communication. The issue is as often a lack of communication regarding successes as it is communication regarding failures, interestingly enough.

It is important to stress that these communications should not simply be between the CIO and the heads of each business unit. By limiting this communication to the most senior levels, a partnering relationship cannot truly be achieved. Communications between the more junior members of teams should also be facilitated. Forums should be created to facilitate them, and more junior members of the IT department should be encouraged to develop training modules designed for peers in the business. This is a good way to spread the understanding of technology while continuing to build a stronger relationship.

I recently worked with a company that had an IT department that was traditionally looked down on by the business. As we used this methodology for the first assessment, the scores that the

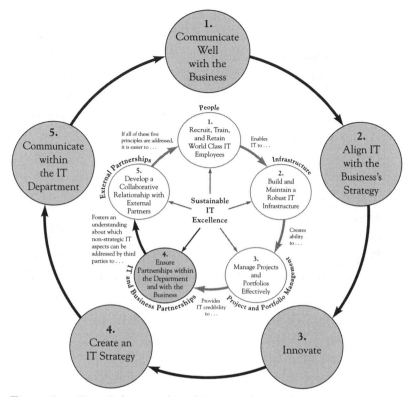

Figure 5.1. Five Subprinciples of Partnership within IT and with the Business.

company received were the lowest we had ever bestowed on any client. When we came back a year later to provide this assessment, the scores relative to IT-business communications and IT-business strategic alignment (which we will cover in the next section) had improved. When we interviewed various business leaders to attempt to find out why, we discovered that many of the SVPs who led the business units pointed again and again to the same manager within the IT department who happened to lead some of the most important IT programs. These programs were highly visible, and this manager was regularly in touch with business leaders. He had recently been hired from a truly World Class IT department. He had taken for granted that he needed to treat IT as a partner rather than act as a mere vendor to the business. Therefore, rather than take his cues from his colleagues who generally did not deign to approach business colleagues as peers, he did so. As a result of this combination of the prominence of the programs that he oversaw with his ability to consult and advise business partners, he had personally caused several business partners to have a change of heart regarding the value that IT could deliver. As a manager, this IT associate was three levels below the CIO, proving that one need not be a member of the IT leadership in order to make a major impact on the business. (It should be noted that this associate was promoted relatively early in his tenure with the company as a result of his work.)

People clearly have a big role to play in IT communications with the business, but one must not underestimate the role that process and tools play. By process, I am referring to developing a process to ensure that there is a regular rhythm to communications. Having empathetic, business-savvy IT associates is important, but counting on them to communicate at all the right times by chance is foolish. There should be set meetings at multiple levels of the IT and business hierarchy to ensure that a constant and consistent flow of information is achieved.

Likewise, developing tools to facilitate this process is also helpful. I believe that many IT departments have a marketing problem insomuch as they do not broadcast their accomplishments well enough. An IT department should set up shared sites within the corporate intranet, for instance, to broadcast points related to IT strategy, IT accomplishments, new hires, promotions, and the like. This should be framed in a way to encourage business associates to read through these, since this will help to broadcast the unique aspects of IT to a greater extent.

Also, IT employees should selectively use email as a way of communicating with the business. Frankly, as I speak with CIOs and their colleagues I suggest reducing the flow of email rather than increasing it, simply because there is a tendency to send too many emails. If the flow of emails is reduced to include only those that are of highest priority, then business associates (to say nothing of IT associates) will tend to read a greater percentage of them rather than simply deleting emails of value because they are the exception rather than the rule.

To this end, we recommend having a biweekly or monthly email that provides an overview of what the IT department has been working on of note in the past period. It should include project updates, as well as metrics showing accomplishments or lack thereof. Where work has fallen short, it would be appropriate to provide a reason behind this as well. It is best to tailor communications to specific business audiences, for instance sending updates on the IT project portfolio for a given business unit to associates in that business unit only.

Subprinciple 2. Align IT with the Business's Strategy

In the late 1990s, I worked as a consultant to one of the major airlines. My first client at the airline was the SVP and CIO, who had a great reputation as a solid IT executive. At the time that I met him, he was accomplishing a lot for the airline, but he was curious if the multiple hundreds of millions of dollars that were in his budget were truly accomplishing what the business needed. Upon further review, we realized that part of the problem was that the business units had not articulated a business plan that was digestible by the IT department.

Many IT executives shy away from these sorts of questions because they are bound to surface answers that may be troubling, and they may lead to significant changes. Undaunted, my client pressed on and convinced the heads of a couple of business units to pilot a process that my team and I designed for him. We developed a three-year strategic plan for that single business unit and then evaluated whether the portfolio of projects directed toward that business unit was, in fact, supporting the newly articulated strategic vision. There were some projects that did not align well, and those were cut. For those that did align well, this provided further justification for continuing them. In addition, there were aspects of the strategic plan that were not covered by the existing portfolio, and the CIO and his team began to design solutions to address those. All the while, the business unit head was impressed to find that the CIO was acting as an agent for strategic change. Once this structure was in place, my client used the plan as a primary means of communicating with the business unit heads, providing regular updates on progress made relative to the projects in the portfolio. As the strategic plan was modified, his portfolio would adjust with it.

After the success of the pilot, business executives who had been reluctant to have an IT-led team help them develop a three-year strategic plan were clamoring for it. In the end, IT's reputation within the business was bolstered all the more.

As my client advanced this process, his team became all the more consultative to the business liaisons with whom they interacted. Again, it is important that all IT associates be engaged in this exercise.

Subprinciple 3. Innovate

The IT department is a natural place for innovation to reside, so long as the leadership is in sync with the business leadership's priorities. This is the key to ensuring that IT leaders are not investing in technology for technology's sake. (This is a criticism that is often cynically leveled against IT departments, and it was an especially popular critique in the early part of this decade during the dot.com bubble.) Strategic innovation is likely to be driven by the business, but innovative solutions should be the domain of the IT department.

This is the primary rationale for innovation to follow on the heels of IT-business strategic alignment. The IT department must understand the objectives that the business has set for itself, and then it must design alternative solutions to assist the business in accomplishing its objectives.

There is an emerging trend of innovation being more formally joined with the IT department. This is personified by Tim Stanley, who, by the end of his tenure at Harrah's Entertainment held not only the title of SVP and CIO but also Head of Innovation. (For good measure, he also led Gaming Operations.)

Stanley succeeded an IT legend in John Boushy. Boushy had also held simultaneous product and IT responsibilities, thus embodying the sort of alignment that most IT departments take great pains to achieve. It was under Boushy's leadership that many of the innovations related to customer relationship management (CRM) were enacted. As a result of Boushy's time as CIO, Harrah's business units took for granted that IT was a source of tremendous value for the business.

It was important, therefore, that his successor be someone who could embody the same sort of principles. Tim Stanley was cut from the same cloth. To meet Stanley is to meet someone who is able to speak about business needs and IT solutions with equal ease. He does not speak using technical jargon, and is quite familiar with concepts such as return on investment that elude some CIOs. As Gary Loveman, chairman and CEO of Harrah's put it, "Tim is a rare technologist in that he is focused not only on our core technology operations but also in ensuring that we leverage technology to address the key value of our company—providing unparalleled guest experiences for our customers."[1]

Stanley was tasked to lead the Innovation team at Harrah's. Stanley has noted that keys to his team's success in setting up this new group were articulating an innovation strategy, developing a roadmap, and putting together a team of Harrah's associates and external partners to rapidly conceive, test, and validate both incremental innovations and "big ideas" and then commercialize them via several parallel innovation tracks and strategic initiatives rapidly, iteratively, and successfully.

One of Stanley's recommendations on setting an IT department up for success in innovation is as follows. "The best way to fast-track a promising innovation ... is to operate it as an independent venture, separate from the tethers of everyday business processes. That often means running an innovation project on separate IT systems to avoid mingling experimental data with business operations." Interestingly enough, when asked why the CIO is a logical candidate to run innovation, he pointed to IT's discipline as one of the key drivers. "A lot of this job is making sure there isn't duplication of effort," he says. "It requires corralling and driving forward. IT is known for process management, and it's arguably better at it than other groups."[2] IT innovation need not be limited to those areas in which the business has identified its needs and objectives through its strategic planning process. However, as with thought process around developing building blocks elsewhere, if IT departments do not already have a long history of innovating on behalf of the business, IT-driven innovation that is outside the confines of the strategic plan may be viewed cynically by the business. Therefore, just as IT executives must prove that they can run their own shop efficiently before they can truly consult the business and participate in the development of their strategic plans, likewise, CIOs should focus on innovating within the confines of the strategic plans generated by the corporation and the business units before seeking innovations that push the envelope. Frankly, if IT is focused on innovations that are too bold before the infrastructure is operating at an appropriate level of reliability, then the innovations themselves are likely to underwhelm because people may need to be pulled from these initiatives to fight the fires related to infrastructure, and at a minimum, IT leadership's attention will be divided.

It is also important to contemplate the people component of innovation. Some innovations may occur to people as an "ah-ha!" moment in the shower, but the most innovative companies dedicate people and time to the innovation process. 3M famously allowed all employees to spend as much as 15 percent of their time on innovations, and they would not necessarily need to report what they were working on or with whom they were working. Many game-changing innovations without any logical predecessor, such as the Post-It Note, were created as a result. The company had a high tolerance for failure because the successes were so great. In the late 1990s, the pace of innovation slowed, and the percentage of revenues derived from new products eroded. As a result, in December of 2000, the company hired James McNerney from General Electric to help the company become more structured.

General Electric is famous for its use of Six Sigma, which is a process invented by Bill Smith of Motorola in 1986 to standardize the way defects are counted.[3] McNerney introduced two basic tools:

- DMAIC, which stands for: define, measure, analyze, improve, control. These five steps are the essence of the Six Sigma approach to problem solving.

- Design for Six Sigma, or DFSS, which systematizes new product development so that Six Sigma quality can be achieved from the outset.

In the first half of the 2000s, 3M's profitability shot up dramatically, and Six Sigma was given a lot of the credit for systematizing the way in which innovation happens. This implementation was not without issues, however, as it was a culture shock to the traditionally process-light (at least from an innovation perspective) company.[4]

This is an example from the company at large, not just the IT department, but these lessons can be applied to the IT department more specifically. It suggests the advantages of structure to the innovation process. As Darko Hrelic, the SVP and CIO of Gartner puts it, anyone looking to innovate should step back and ask, "what are the needs of the business?" This is what innovation should revolve around. Hrelic contends that "even pure research organizations cannot innovate solely for the sake of innovating any more."[5]

Rob Austin, associate professor of technology and operations management at Harvard Business School, indicates that IT departments need to develop the ability to "trystorm."[6] By this he refers to developing new ideas, and trying them quickly and cheaply, being willing to quickly cancel the projects if they prove not to be as interesting as they were earlier believed to be.

One of Rob Austin's colleagues at Harvard Business School, Michael Tushman, and Mary Benner, who is an assistant professor of management at Wharton, published a study of technology innovation in which they concluded that a balance needs to be struck between innovation through a well-honed process and what the authors refer to as "exploration," which involves more technical and innovative experimentation. They write that process management practices "can tip the balance toward incremental innovation in organizations through two main mechanisms—through incremental learning, as process management activities are increasingly applied to an organization's routines, and through their influence on the internal selection environment for innovation projects. Both of these mechanisms tend to favor exploitation at the expense of exploration as organizations incrementally improve innovation processes and short-term, easy-to-measure efficiency improvements make vague, uncertain, difficult-to-quantify exploratory activities less attractive." They point out that this works well in stable environments, but in industries where competitors rapidly innovate, this may be a dangerous path to go down.

They conclude their article by saying, "Organizations can resolve these contradictions by adopting ambidextrous organizational designs that enable them to pursue exploitation and exploration simultaneously. In an ambidextrous organization, exploration units succeed by experimenting while exploitation units succeed by reducing variability and maximizing efficiency and control. By being ambidextrous, organizations can develop processes for establishing new, forward-looking cognitive models for exploration units, while allowing backward-looking experiential learning to rapidly unfold for exploitation units."[7]

This is generally sound advice. Many World Class IT departments have chosen to pursue a hybrid approach. In so doing, they dedicate a portion of the team to innovation so that they can begin to build the necessary skills.

There are now creative tools that can be used to help foster the process of generating new, innovative ideas. Many companies, including Dell and Starbucks, have used Salesforce.com's online voting services called Ideas to uncover new innovative opportunities. Employees and customers can use these services, typically accessed through the company's website, to submit new ideas and vote on the best new ideas. Dell developed a Linux-based laptop, and Starbucks came up with a well-publicized promotion for a free cup of coffee for anyone who voted on Starbucks innovations, both using these services.[8] Therefore, IT has a role to play in fostering innovation by providing the tools as well as by helping to generate the ideas that will become the new innovative products, services, and promotions of tomorrow.

Subprinciple 4. Create an IT Strategy

Optimally, IT strategy and business strategy should be part of the same plan. Most of an IT department's activities should align with the objectives of the corporation and the business units. As these plans are developed, IT associates should provide guidance and feedback, and even take steps to help mold these plans as appropriate. It becomes that much easier for the IT department to then recommend the solutions that will help realize the vision articulated through the business strategy.

Once all of the business strategic plans have been articulated, it is important for IT associates to look through each of them and consider what themes emerge out of them. For instance, customer relationship management (CRM) is an undertaking that can have an impact on many parts of the company. It provides data for Marketing to troll for insights on how to segment customers, and how to market products or services based on what they learn about the customers. It can help different product or service areas identify all the products or services each client uses. This unified view may lead to different conclusions about who the most valuable clients are, and how they can be treated differently. Any one of these areas might have trouble justifying what can be a very hefty investment in IT, but if IT leaders can see that this is a theme that is emerging out of several parts of the business, the CIO can present to the board and senior leadership for a global solution to CRM. This will ensure that it is done once and done correctly with the entire company in mind. This is not something that each of the parts of the business would necessarily see themselves; given the IT department's perch in the corporation, IT members are well positioned to see these themes emerging.

With principle 2, we also covered infrastructure, and mentioned that this is an area that is typically the domain of the IT department alone. The business is not likely to advise the IT department on the need for infrastructure changes. Those conversations have to happen in the reverse. As a result, once all of the business plans are in place, and once the various subprinciple items related to infrastructure (such as the infrastructure roadmap, retirement, disaster recovery, or business continuity) are instituted, the IT department will be in a better position to articulate its IT strategy.

IT strategy development should not be limited to as exclusive a club as is typically the case. To have the entire IT department understand and support the IT strategy, a larger percentage of people need to feel they have had a role to play in its creation, and everyone must feel as though they have a role to play in its execution. As W. Chan Kim and Renée Mauborgne suggest in their seminal book on strategy, *Blue Ocean Strategy: How to Create Uncontested Market Space and Make the Competition Irrelevant*, "In the end, a company needs to invoke the most fundamental base of action: the attitudes and behavior of its people deep in the organization. You must create a culture of trust and commitment that motivates people to execute the agreed strategy—not to the letter, but to the spirit. People's minds and hearts must align with the new strategy so that at the level of the individual, people embrace it of their own accord and willingly go beyond compulsory execution to voluntary cooperation in carrying it out."[9]

Inherent in these ideas is that there needs to be a bottom-up aspect to strategic planning. This does not suggest that all of IT should be engaged at the point at which there is a blank slate. On the contrary, that would be a risky formula, as ideas would be offered with little structure, and the initial excitement of being engaged in an important process for the company would yield to feelings of disappointment as most people's ideas would not be considered. Instead, the creation of the highest-level objectives is still probably the domain of IT leadership. The tactics on how to accomplish each should be the domain of the larger organization. The objectives provide the structure, and the tactics provide a list of ideas to which the organization can turn when a new round of project ideas are needed.

The plan must be written in plain English. Often strategy documents either have esoteric language that is only understandable to a small cadre of the most senior leaders, or they are sufficiently vague as to render them meaningless. It is important that plans be written with the goal of making them understandable to someone who was not privy to their creation.

By both engaging the entire organization in the creation of the strategy and documenting the strategy in language that everyone can understand, the organization will go a long way toward ensuring that people will adhere to and ultimately push the strategy forward to completion.

Subprinciple 5. Communicate within the IT Department

Once IT leadership has worked with the business to understand its needs, and once the people deeper in the IT organization develop stronger ties with business partners, it is critical that cross-IT communications become focal. Several of my client organizations' IT leaders get along well, share information well, and develop plans together well, and yet the different parts of the IT organizations that they lead do not work so well together. For some reason the strong relationships at the top do not translate down.

IT communications are sometimes lost in the details as IT departments push to align themselves with the business. The traditional breakdown is between development and maintenance or support. The first group develops new technologies, and the second group must support those technologies. Too often, development develops its programs in a vacuum without involving maintenance, and then throws the new software over the proverbial wall for maintenance to maintain. A lot of time is then wasted as those in maintenance must learn what they have just received. Suggestions that could have been made to make the software easier to maintain are now moot.

A key to ensure that IT communications flow more efficiently is to have people rotate through different parts of IT. This provides a greater level of understanding across the group, but it also will lead to better ideas on how to continue to improve the dialogue and information flow.

It is also appropriate to have representatives from all departments of IT present in the early stages of the development of projects. That way, if a new development does not take into account the support needs, those concerns can be voiced at the point when changes can still be made.

Metrics

As with the "people" metrics, the measurement of alignment across the IT department and between the department and the business is often done through polling the different constituents. I have found that many IT departments do not do enough of this internal surveying, nor do they poll their internal customers to a great enough extent.

Improvements in these metrics will ultimately prove the value of IT (Table 5.1). As IT employees believe they are working together effectively, productivity and job satisfaction will increase. As the business's opinion of its relationship with the IT department improves and their perceptions of the quality of what IT produces improves, IT will, by definition, be adding greater levels of value to the corporation.

Table 5.1.   Metrics for Ensuring That IT Partners within the Department and with the Business.

Subprinciple	Introductory Metrics	Advanced Metrics
Communicate Well with the Business	• Number of quarterly IT-business strategy meetings • Percentage of business decision makers in regular contact with IT counterparts • IT-business survey result scores	• Percentage of IT-business miscommunication issues resolved • Response rate to business versus IT requests • Percentage of cross-functional career changes

Table 5.1. Metrics for Ensuring That IT Partners within the Department and with the Business. (Continued)

Subprinciple	Introductory Metrics	Advanced Metrics
Communicate Well with the Business, cont'd.	• Business-IT survey result scores	• Number of non-business staff on business team or non-IT on IT team
		• Number or percentage of common IT and business competencies (in job descriptions or evaluations)
Align IT with the Business's Strategy	• Percentage of IT budget spent on business priorities (and vice versa)	• Percentage of the business's IT priorities met by IT
	• Number of applications used by more than one line of business	• IT and business satisfaction survey improvements
	• Ratio of decisions made by IT and business leader over X period	• Assessment of the understanding of the other function
	• Number or percentage of IT versus business-sponsored activities	• Ratio of business and IT priorities relative to overall priorities
	• Ratio of common to functional success or performance metrics	• Percentage of consensus decisions relative to total number of decisions

Table 5.1. *(Continued)*

Subprinciple	Introductory Metrics	Advanced Metrics
Innovate	• Number of products or services launched in X period • R&D spending as percentage of sales • Percentage of project ideas generated by IT department versus the business • Customer satisfaction with new products or new services	• Percentage of business challenges solved by IT • Revenue growth (dollars or percentage) over X period from new products or new services • Return on investment from new products or services • Net present value from new product or services portfolio • Change in market share as result of new products or services
Create an IT Strategy	• Percentage of IT staff that understands direction of IT • Percentage of IT-specific projects aligned with IT strategy	• Number or percentage of IT strategies aligned to business strategies • Degree of IT strategy linkage to corporate or business strategies

Table 5.1.   Metrics for Ensuring That IT Partners within the Department and with the Business. *(Continued)*

Subprinciple	Introductory Metrics	Advanced Metrics
Communicate within the IT Department	• Percentage of shared ideas and resources across IT • Number of quarterly cross-IT strategy meetings	• Percentage of IT staff with strong understanding of other parts of the IT department

IT's Partnering with the Company and Its Broader Company Role

This is the principle through which IT touches the rest of the business. It is in many ways the most important of the principles. As mentioned earlier, the first three principles are foundational, and if they are not operating at a high level, then it will be impossible for IT to establish a true partnering relationship with the business. It is also important to separate out the other part of this principle, however: if IT does not establish a partnering relationship across the IT department itself, it certainly will not be an effective partner to the business either.

When the IT department operates this principle at a high level, this is where the greatest value can be achieved. IT departments that align well with the business, developing capabilities that align with their needs and priorities will be the most successful.

6

Principle 5: Develop a Collaborative Relationship with External Partners

Outsourcing to external partners has increased so much that I focus this last, large principle on it. I believe it is now an important weapon in the arsenals of most CIOs at medium or large companies. I present it last because it follows logically from the previous chapter about IT and business partnerships. Under principle 4, the CIO works with the business to understand that which is strategic and that which is not. Under the fifth principle, the CIO and his team can determine which of the aspects of IT that are not strategic can be outsourced.

Among larger IT departments, outsourcing makes a lot of sense. External partners can lend skills that current staff do not possess, they can be used to fill in teams when other team members are not available, and they can be used to take over entire functions within the IT department.

Also, an increasing number of "off the shelf" solutions are cheaper and easier to implement than developing a comparable technology internally. Anyone with some experience with Microsoft Excel could build a personal accounting database to track spending. Since there are other sophisticated and relatively cheap products, such as Intuit's QuickBooks, that one can purchase, the time spent building the spreadsheets through Excel would not be time well spent.

IT departments engage individual contractors, and they engage firms. These individuals and firms may be on-site, or they may operate half a world away. From my experience, I have found that outsourcing has outpaced the development of processes to govern these relationships. Therefore, many companies do not get nearly enough out of their external partners. This part of the book will address that problem.

Some Broad Considerations

Before going into details of the principle, some discussion is in order about outsourcing and your department's readiness to do it.

First Get Your Own House in Order

Whenever I work with a company that has been underwhelmed by the performance of key external partners, I ask about the company's own internal processes related to people (principle 1) and project and portfolio management (principle 3). If IT leaders do not do a good job of evaluating their own people, promoting and showing appreciation for the high performers, and taking the necessary action with the low performers, they are not likely to push their external partners to do likewise with their people. And if the IT team does not have a solid project development lifecycle, and if the portfolio is not tracked to see which projects are on time, on budget, and on scope, then it is almost impossible for the company to effectively govern the external partner.

Why Companies Outsource—Reasons Good and Bad

Many companies in the United States and other countries have outsourced development work in order to gain cost advantages with firms in places such as India, China, and Eastern Europe. Those who quickly engaged external partners around the globe, or "offshore" as it is often described, for the purposes of saving money have been burned, however. For this reason, I believe that companies should avoid outsourcing development for cost advantage alone. Many companies that have made major commitments to offshore operations simply on the basis of cost advantages have not actually achieved savings, as the cost of doing business in many of these locations has risen or at least fluctuated a great deal over the past few years.

Many companies look for an advantage in twenty-four-hour-a-day development, given that an offshore operation in India, for instance, is working while headquarters in the United States is closed, and vice versa. This suggests cutting up projects and having people in both locations work on the same project, but our research has led us to conclude that there is tremendous inefficiency in working in this way. When projects are cut up and collaboration deteriorates due to differing time schedules, much is lost in translation. You end up needing to figure out what the other party just did, and because they are asleep now you cannot ask them and get a quick answer. Assumptions are made, sometimes incorrectly, and time is wasted as a result.

Hazards and Payoffs of Massive Outsourcing

It is probably not surprising that the larger the outsourcing contract and the broader its scope, the more difficult it is to manage and the more risk there is. Engaging one independent contractor is not likely to be too expensive, nor will he or she be difficult to release if value is not realized. Signing up a multiyear and multimillion dollar contract to outsource a major portion of IT is a different story. One must think about the people, processes, tools, metrics, and culture of that firm, and determine how they fit with the people, processes, tools, metrics and culture of your own company. It is not possible that there will be a perfect fit between the two, but it is the differences that will in many ways determine whether the relationship will be successful or not.

One prominent company that effectively outsourced its entire IT department is Best Buy, a leading consumer electronics retailer in the United States. Robert Willett, who holds the joint title of CEO of Best Buy International and chief information officer (how is that for business alignment, incidentally?), is a *CIO* magazine Hall of Famer for his work in retail in many different areas. He has a nontraditional background; having started as a store manager at Marks & Spencer in the United Kingdom, he rose to become the global managing partner for the retail practice at Accenture. Willett joined Best Buy as a special adviser to the board on matters relating to operational efficiency and excellence. He joined the company permanently in 2003 as the executive vice president of operations. Retail, generally, is an industry with low margins, and therefore it is important to understand where dollars can be saved in order to affect the bottom line. Willett realized that it would be possible to save a great deal of money while focusing more on modifying business processes than on software. Many retailers have grown up building all of their own software, and multiple clients of ours in the industry have used terms such as *hairball* to describe the way the infrastructure is structured (or not, more likely). Willett recognized there was value in having an outside firm worry about unwinding the complicated proprietary systems and building a new, more efficient infrastructure, and he initiated the process of outsourcing IT to Accenture and other major vendors.

Of the 820 people in the IT department, roughly 650 received offers from Accenture, 130 were laid off, and 40 were left to oversee IT strategy and manage the Accenture relationship, and the relationships with other firms that were brought in. Best Buy would still determine which ideas IT should pursue, but these would be fulfilled by external partners. Also, the contract was wisely written, with explicit service-level agreements and business outcomes spelled out.[1]

Willett was able to anticipate the people, process, tools, metrics, and culture issues by having gotten to know both companies in the transaction as an insider. Therefore, he had a foot in both of the worlds that he needed to lead and could anticipate a lot of the challenges to a better degree than most.

Willett is very clear in defining the value that one should expect to gain through a large-scale, strategic outsourcing event. He says that those who pursue this strategy only to save money are bound to be disappointed. Given the complexity of this sort of undertaking, it is quite possible that it will be a long time before a company can truly realize cost savings. Rather, Willett provides the following reasons in order of priority:

1. Increase pace of change
2. Bring new capabilities to the business
3. Access new skills when they are needed
4. Reduce risk
5. Reduce your cost[2]

Note that cost savings are the last factor listed. Willett instead has indicated that more value will be gained through speed, efficiency, and flexibility that the model provides.

When I first spoke with Bob Willett about this very topic, I asked him whether he ever worried that using firms that his competitors might also use could mean that innovations might decrease, or that other companies might have all the same ideas his did. He responded cleverly by saying that many Formula One race cars are alike, but the champions know how to drive them better. Furthermore, he notes that his IT leaders, whom he refers to as business information officers, or BIOs, are responsible for working with the business to identify new sources of innovation. The external partners simply fulfill these requests.[3]

What Successful Outsourcing Requires

Offshore operations do very much have their merits, but I have found them most successful if the outsourcing company has done the following:

- Have a member of the corporate IT department spend a significant amount of time on the operation during set up.
  - This person will ensure that the operation runs smoothly.
  - He or she can teach the new external partners about the parent organization.
  - He or she can bring a bit of the culture of the parent organization to the new offshore entity while allowing it to maintain those aspects that are unique and special.
- Ensure that there is a strong leader and point person who is optimally dedicated to the work.
  - Given the complexity of work in a different part of the globe, it is easiest if there is one primary point of contact.
  - That does not mean that other people on the team should not be contacted. On the contrary, it can be very motivating to staff to hear from members of the parent organization.
- Find a work stream that the operation can own in its entirety.
  - This helps solve the aforementioned inefficiency.
  - Business requirements still need to be defined by internal resources, but once defined, development through to quality assurance should be done by the offshore team.
- Set up well-articulated performance metrics, including service-level agreements (SLAs).

- I will go through the need for SLAs later in this chapter, but it is absolutely critical that they be well articulated, understood, and monitored.
- Deviations from the SLAs should have consequences, as should performance that exceeds the SLAs.

- Try to arrange to pay based on deliverables and therefore value rather than time.

This last point is worth a longer look. The traditional way of pricing is based on time spent, an inefficient method that actually means the client's and external partner's goals are not aligned. The external partner has an incentive to bill more hours to make more money. This not only means more expense for the client, it also creates an incentive for lateness.

A trend has emerged among several World Class IT departments. Given the difficulty in monitoring hour-to-hour and day-to-day performance of an operation that is in many cases a hemisphere away, paying based on deliverables and value can ensure that everyone focuses on the right metrics, and that incentives are aligned. The external partner will have higher margins by eliminating as much wasted effort as possible, but because value can be translated into quality, they must be sure that the product runs to specifications.

Phaneesh Murthy is the president and CEO of iGATE Corporation, which is a provider of IT and offshore outsourcing services to large and medium-sized organizations. Murthy's prior experience includes a stint as the head of global sales and marketing at Infosys. He has been at the forefront of offshoring since before it was a prominent term in most people's business lexicon. Murthy is very blunt when he speaks about the average IT outsourcer. According to Murthy, "For too long, the [IT outsourcing] industry has taken advantage of customers.... Through the [past] twenty or thirty years, in effect the pricing models have not changed dramatically.... There is an incentive in most companies to be mildly inefficient as long as the customer doesn't catch it." To align the incentives, Murthy has incorporated a philosophy at his company to charge on the basis of outcome rather than effort. "The customer should only pay for the results that they achieve," says Murthy.[4]

This is the true essence of establishing external partnerships as opposed to simply client-vendor relationships. No matter the type of outsourcing relationship, it is important to understand the objectives of the undertaking and the value anticipated, but it is also important for the client company to think about how success is defined for external partners as well. We will explore this in more depth when we cover the subprinciple on procurement.

Each year, *Computer Economics* publishes a report on outsourcing trends. The findings of the 2008 report read as follows:[5]

1. *Application development.* Outsourcing where a service provider is responsible for developing new systems. Application development is the most popular form of outsourcing, in use by 53% of the organizations in our study.

2. *Application maintenance.* Outsourcing where a service provider takes over the maintenance of existing systems. Outsourcing of application maintenance is practiced by 44% of the organizations in our study.

3. *Website or e-commerce systems.* Outsourcing where a third party develops, hosts, or maintains a corporate website (Internet or intranet) or e-commerce system. This form of outsourcing is quite popular, in use by about 40% of the organizations in our study.

4. *Disaster recovery services.* Outsourcing where an outside provider is responsible for offsite data storage, recovery data centers, or redundant systems or networks that are used in the

event of a disaster or other disruption requiring business continuity services. This function is outsourced by 37% of the organizations in our study.

5. *Data center operations*. Outsourcing where data centers are managed and operated by an outside service provider. This includes data centers where facilities or computer hardware are owned by the customer, as well as cases where data centers or computer equipment are owned by the service provider. This form of outsourcing is practiced by about one third of organizations.

6. *Data network operations*. Outsourcing where a service provider is responsible for all or part of data network operations, network monitoring, or contract services to install, repair, or maintain data network equipment, software, or circuits. This form of outsourcing is in use by about one third of the organizations in our study.

7. *Voice network operations*. Outsourcing where a service provider is responsible for all or part of voice network operations, network monitoring, or contract services to install, repair, or maintain voice network equipment, software, or circuits. It is practiced by 30% of our respondents.

8. *Help desk*. Outsourcing where an outside provider is responsible for any type of first-level phone or electronic response to end-user incidents or inquiries. This form of outsourcing is practiced by 28% of the organizations in our study.

9. *IT security*. Outsourcing where an outside provider provides security-related services, such as security assessments, penetration testing, or managed security services. Only about one-quarter of organizations are using outside service providers for IT security.

10. *Desktop support.* Outsourcing where a service provider is responsible for acquisition, installation, maintenance, or support of desktop or laptop computers. This form of outsourcing is practiced by about one-quarter of our respondents.

11. *Database administration.* Outsourcing where the outside provider is used to develop, monitor, and tune databases, at the physical or logical level. This form of outsourcing is practiced by about one-quarter of organizations.

What Not to Outsource

Following are some of the main types of work that should not be outsourced:

- *Business analysis.* This is nearly impossible to outsource. It is critical that IT associates work with business associates to identify needs and architect solutions. Those solutions may well be developed by someone else, but external partners are unlikely to understand the strategy and the needs of the business as IT colleagues would.

- *Enterprise architecture.* It is also important that a group of people in the IT department own the enterprise architecture function. These are the people who should track the infrastructure roadmap and understand how the different moving pieces that are developed by IT department staff and external partners all fit together. Unless the entire department is outsourced, this is not something that should be left to someone at another firm.

- *Project management.* This skill must be applied as ably externally as it is internally. If a company does not have sound project management processes, and a stable of solid project managers, then it should not embark on any significant outsourcing. Ultimately, external partners are people, and they have competing demands among the clients for whom they work. It is only human nature that they will work hardest for those who push them the hardest. When an external partner engages with a company that does not have project managers overseeing their work, and that does not have a sound project management process with stage gates and hurdles through which projects must pass and be tracked, they are likely to focus more attention to those that do. A lack of project management translates into a lack of oversight, and external partners naturally will focus more attention to those companies that are overseeing their activities at a more granular level.

- *Portfolio management.* Likewise, this must remain part of the domain of IT associates. Projects may be run by associates and by external partners, but the entire portfolio must be tracked through dashboards, and when projects begin to deviate from plans, alarms should sound and action should be taken to rectify the issues. Unless all of IT has been outsourced, this cannot be a function left to the external partner to manage.

- *Release management.* This means monitoring when new technologies should be implemented or "released" to the users for whom they were intended, and also must be managed internally. This becomes much more complex when a portion of the portfolio is developed by external partners. Just as portfolio management cannot be managed externally because only an IT associate can have the global perspective, the same logic applies to release management: only an IT associate can determine the timing when different technologies can be released so that there is not too much stress put on the system by having too much released at once.

- *Vendor management.* Perhaps somewhat obviously, this also must be managed internally. Having one external partner manage another pits third parties against each other.

Three Subprinciples of External Partnering

For companies that have not traditionally engaged external partners to those who do so frequently, Figure 6.1 captures three subprinciples to follow.

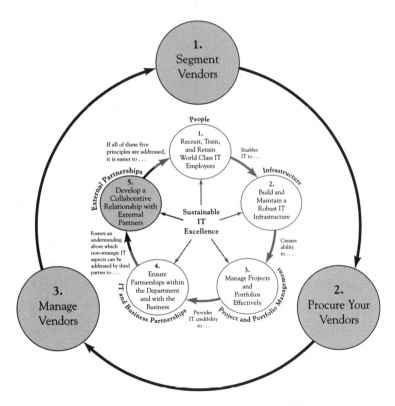

Figure 6.1. Three Subprinciples for External Partnering.

Subprinciple 1. Segment Vendors

Outsourcing can be defined in two broad important segments: strategic outsourcing and staff augmentation, each of which is divisible into subcategories.

External partners who provide strategic services are those who take ownership over entire projects or even take over functions on behalf of the IT department, as the earlier examples suggest. Staff augmentation partners offer skills that probably exist internally but in short supply. They are not brought on for thought leadership (at least as a primary role). Rather, typically they are brought on as additional arms, legs, and minds for a project.

Although staff augmentation partners may seem mundane compared to strategic ones, World Class IT departments think about augmentation as a key weapon in their arsenal. For instance, some IT departments overstaff during good years, and they must prune that staff during lean years. More wisely, World Class IT departments foresee and expect historical shifts—waxing and waning of business cycles—and they plan accordingly. As a result, when a downturn hits, they are better able to let go external partners for a time, but not decimate their permanent staff.

A first step in the vendor segmentation process is to take an inventory of all external partners currently engaged.

1. Document the tenure of the relationship.
2. Document the trajectory of the relationship.
   - Positive trend and why
   - Negative trend and why
3. Evaluate the quality of the following characteristics of the external partner. These should then become the criteria on which potential external partners are evaluated, as well.
   - Client knowledge
   - Industry knowledge

- Leadership
- Staff in general
- Specific skills or roles related to the processes or technologies that they oversee
- Cultural fit

4. Adherence to service level agreements

Results should be tallied as on a scorecard for all relevant external partners and published for them to see (each external partner sees its own company named but not the names of the other companies).

This should be done on a quarterly or even a monthly basis, giving external partners who are engaged for many months at a time a chance to course correct before the conclusion of their engagement with the company.

Subprinciple 2. Procure Your Vendors

Procurement (or sourcing, as it is often called) is a specialized part of the process to engage external partners. This function was created so that there would be trained negotiators who could engage potential external partners, typically prior to signing a contract.

Just as sports agents are often engaged to speak harshly about the team that a player plays for so that the player need not do so, the procurement function plays this same role. Negotiators can engage in tough conversations before the contract is signed, and once it is, they can fade to the background.

Sometimes this function is performed by the IT department, especially for companies that have a heavy emphasis on technology, and sometimes this is an independent shared service in the corporation. If the latter is the case, the IT department must push to ensure that there be a dedicated person or people for IT, and that the person who is dedicated have some background in IT. Having regularly dealt with procurement departments as part of my role, I know there is nothing more frustrating for a new external partner than negotiating with someone who knows nothing about technology.

As Murthy says, "The contracting process has to undergo the most massive amount of re-engineering.... Where Sourcing [procurement] is more business led, it is a lot easier to make these changes to put together agreements where there are high degrees of trust and mutual gain." He refers to traditional contracts as "beat up" contracts, and says that procurement needs to focus on providing incentives for external partners to provide the highest degree of value possible. The best contracts he has seen have provided possible gains for the external partner for new innovative ideas brought to the client company or shared benefit for cost savings derived from the work. These are truly win-win scenarios.[6]

Subprinciple 3. Manage Vendors

In recognition of the importance of sound vendor management functions, many World Class IT departments have vendor management offices (VMOs). Members of the VMO oversee the processes of managing the external partners, even though they may not literally manage all of the partners. They monitor the work of the vendors, they maintain scorecards, and they oversee external partner evaluations.

Members of the VMO may manage the largest external partnerships, but they typically relegate day-to-day management of smaller or specialized engagements to the relevant departments. The VMO is typically responsible for aggregating information for regular (typically quarterly and annual) vendor reviews. These should be quantitative and qualitative, and the success metrics should be known to the vendors ahead of time, so that they know where they should be aiming. Vendors typically like this because it gives them a gauge of progress, or lack thereof, and it gives them the opportunity to course correct should they need to do so. Obviously, vendors don't want to be surprised to know that they are not meeting expectations, especially if it is at the point at which it is too late and the client organization has chosen to engage a competitor.

Many VMOs choose to rank vendors and then publish those rankings, and provide awards for those at the top. This creates a positive peer pressure among the vendors.

Vendor management is the responsibility of many people who engage external partners, not just those people who populate the VMO or who run the vendor management function for the IT department. The VMO or heads of vendor management should also be responsible for training all relevant people on sound vendor management skills. They should ensure that all relevant parties are familiar with the contract that governs the relationship with the external partner with whom they interact, and that all SLAs are known. They should ensure that success metrics are monitored on a regular basis. They also should be trained on relationship building, given how important it is to maintain relationships with external partners, especially strategic ones.

Many World Class IT departments publish their business strategies for key strategic external partners to see. If they are truly strategic, then they should be cognizant of the strategy. That way, they can suggest where they can be helpful. Some IT employees chafe at this suggestion, arguing that it will only lead to more attempts by the external partners to sell work, but why shouldn't these external partners attempt to sell work so long as it is germane to the business's plan? If they can connect the dots between their areas of expertise and the needs of the IT department and the business more generally, then, again, this benefits both companies.

Metrics

The metrics associated with external partnerships are important in ensuring that value is generated from the relationship with third parties. These need to be set up at the outset of the relationship (Table 6.1).

Table 6.1. Metrics for Developing a Collaborative Relationship with External Partners.

Subprinciple	Introductory Metrics	Advanced Metrics
Segment Vendors	• Percentage of vendors categorized • Percentage of vendors correctly categorized • Vendor spending level • Scope and real-time business impact of vendor services • Level of use within the company or by end users • Length of relationship by vendor	• Percentage of vendors managed based on assigned category • Vendor scorecard score relative to average score
Procure Your Vendors	• Percentage of contracts with reduced fee structures • Percentage of contracts staying within originally anticipated budget during procurement • Average number of proposals considered before a vendor is chosen • Percentage of IT needs fully met by contracts • Average number of days to procurement from the time a request is received	• Percentage of contracts staying within budget over lifetime of contract • Percentage of contracts maintaining scope and value from beginning to end of procurement process

Table 6.1. Metrics for Developing a Collaborative Relationship with
External Partners. *(Continued)*

Subprinciple	Introductory Metrics	Advanced Metrics
Manage Vendors	• Vendor hourly rates (total or ratio relative to comparable in-house staff) • Vendor contract costs (total or percentage of IT budget) • Percentage change of vendor rates or costs over X period • Percentage of contracts with service-level agreements • Percentage of contracts meeting service-level agreements or business requirements • Percentage of breaches of service recorded • Percentage of external partner contracts carried through without penalties or early termination • Percentage of on-time and on-budget service delivery • Percentage of completion of vendor projects	• Percentage of breaches of service-level agreements penalized • Vendor-provided availability of assets and systems (as percentage or relative to in-house systems) • Vendor agreement renewal rate

Because this is the only principle explicitly dealing with third parties, it is all the more important that metrics be put in place because third parties do not always naturally have the same degree of ownership over the work product delivered to the company as employees do because of the longer-term relationship of the latter.

Like the metrics associated with the second and third principles, these metrics should be easier to quantify, as this does not require surveys. Actual results should be more readily quantifiable, and therefore should also be less disputable as a result.

Many of these metrics should be made available to external partners to let them know how they are performing, where they need to improve, and how they are performing relative to other external partners. Needless to say, this will provide ample motivation for continued improvement. The comparison with other external partners also suggests that scorecards should be made. If the IT department has a vendor management office, these metrics and the creation of the scorecards are likely to be under the purview of the VMO's leaders. If not, this should be the primary task of someone in the IT department, given the importance of this.

External Partnering and IT's Expanded Company Role

As mentioned earlier in this chapter, IT has the opportunity to lead the rest of the organization to better results as it engages external partners because IT departments tend to have more contracts with external partners than any other part of the organization.

Bear in mind that it is necessary to apply several of the subprinciples from the prior chapters externally as well.

People

Inventory existing skills. Just as it is important to understand which skills are in abundance and which are in short supply internally, the same needs to be done externally. This balance or imbalance may uncover the need for additional resources either internally or externally. If this is not done, then the company may be paying for redundant skills when engaging external partners.

Plan your workforce. When reviewing the business strategy, and contemplating new skills that will increasingly be in demand, one way to ramp up those skills is to engage external partners. The urgency of the needs will dictate the pace at which external partners should be engaged. Understanding whether those skills will continue to be in demand will also help highlight whether the company should build those skills internally or simply engage the external partners for a time, and once the need for those skills fades, the partnership (at least as it pertains to the skills in question) can cease.

Clarify titles, roles, and responsibilities. Without articulating clear titles, roles, and responsibilities, then it will be difficult to align the company's hierarchy with the hierarchy of the firms that the company may engage. This is not to say that the company needs to have the same titles, roles, and responsibilities as all of its vendors, nor does it mean that it should dictate that external partners adopt those of the company. Rather, one's titles should not be so esoteric as to not be easily translatable to another organization's titles, roles, and responsibilities.

Evaluate meaningfully. As mentioned earlier, it is critical to provide meaningful evaluations to all external partner organizations, and to let them know how they rank against other companies. Many World Class IT departments take this to the next level of actually providing evaluations of individuals on the external partner's team. This provides a signal to external partners that they cannot simply send below-average vendors to the company and have it go unnoticed. It also helps ensure that these below-average vendors will be replaced with more talented ones. This needs to be worked into contracts, of course. Last, if the external partnership is to be a long-lasting one, then it is in the company's best interest to provide this feedback so that the external partners know who and where to improve.

Recognize and compensate high performance. Recognition is the more important of the two aspects of this subprinciple to external vendors. If individual external partners are to feel as though they are a part of the team, then they should be recognized just as employees are. Good work should be recognized. Some World Class IT departments go so far as to offer the same sorts of awards and prizes to external partners as they do to employees. This blurs the line between employees and external partners, and in most cases that is a good thing.

Infrastructure

Create an infrastructure roadmap. This is as vital a first step internally as it is externally. Without knowledge of the infrastructure roadmap, it will be difficult if not impossible to know how projects that external partners work on or even suggest fit into the overall infrastructure of the company.

Maximize systems' up-time. Monitoring the reliability of systems is key so that when projects undertaken by external partners are released, they are as reliable as other comparable systems. Also, it is critical that the company can prove when system down-time is due to issues related to external partners.

Develop disaster recovery and business continuity plans. As external partners become increasingly interwoven into the fabric of the modern IT department, understanding how to replace an external partner should it be necessary is critically important. World Class IT VMOs or vendor management functions should always have a backup list for all existing external partners so that they can quickly engage or at least request a proposal from a potential external partner should the time come. Likewise, external partners should be pushed to develop business continuity and disaster recovery plans for any function that they own. (Of course other aspects may be relevant depending on what has been outsourced.)

Project and Portfolio Management

Generate ideas. True external partners should be provided incentives to generate new ideas on behalf of the company. This means that they should know how to submit ideas, and they should also become familiar with the criteria used to evaluate new ideas.

Budget. Budgeting takes into account all IT expenditures, and the extent to which a portion of those are spent on external partners should be appropriately factored in the budgeting process.

Manage portfolios. As mentioned before, this is a critical governance hurdle. External partners must know that their projects are being monitored along with all other projects. In some cases, external partners will provide some of the data that are used to track projects for portfolio management.

Manage and execute projects. Also mentioned earlier was the need for sound project management principles and staff to apply to and oversee external partners. Without a logical process in place and staff to oversee external partners' activities, partners may let down their guards. Just as employees should be driven to keep projects on time, on budget, and on scope, so too should external partners.

Ensure quality. External partners should be pushed to ensure that everything they deliver is of the highest quality, meeting the standards set in the service-level agreements. The company must confirm that external partners have an applicable quality assurance process in place.

Review and report performance. External partners must report progress on a regular basis. They should be encouraged to share bad news as early as possible, but at the same time be pushed to articulate potential remedies where applicable.

Analyze after the project is done. All external partners should be included in project postmortems. They should understand what they have done well, and where there is room for improvement.

IT and Business Partnerships

Align IT with the business's strategy. As mentioned before, it is important that at least the most mission-critical strategic partners be cognizant of the company's strategy so that they can suggest areas where they can be helpful, and so they can provide ideas for solutions to meet the business's needs.

Innovate. The best external partners should be given incentives to innovate on behalf of the company. If they are truly strategic partners then they should know enough about the company's plans (through the prior subprinciple) to develop innovative ideas for solutions for the company.

Create an IT strategy. External partners should also comment on and even help guide the IT strategy. If they have gotten to know the company well, then they should understand enough about the plans to at least provide comments on them, suggesting ways in which they can be enhanced.

Communicate within IT. External partners should be one more part of the IT organization across which information should flow. Just as information needs to seamlessly flow from business analysts to project managers to developers to release managers to maintenance, that information should flow to and through the external partners wherever they may operate in that continuum.

Conclusion

There is no question that information technology's prominence is increasing within corporations. In light of this trend, it is incumbent upon IT executives to have a comprehensive way to evaluate how the organization is performing. In which domains is IT succeeding? In which should it strive to improve further? Furthermore, many IT departments perform well for a time but do not sustain that level of performance. Just as thriving companies providing great products and services generate greater levels of demand, so do thriving IT departments. In this very way, many IT departments lose their edge because they outgrow their processes and metrics. As the department grows, so do the project portfolio and the number of people and offices. Relying on a limited number of overtasked people to save the day in a technology-related crisis becomes very risky. It thus is critically important to be able to monitor performance on an ongoing basis.

One might be tempted to quibble with the order and content of the World Class IT principles and subprinciples. They certainly are not mutually exclusive and, as mentioned before, they are not always intended to operate as a continuum, since IT organizations will work on aspects of all five principles every day. What we can say is that, having worked with a wide variety of leading CIOs and IT departments—as well as a handful of industry laggards—this order has made sense to us and to our clients.

Frankly, the order of the World Class IT framework is less important than having a framework that everyone understands. Don't let the perfect be the enemy of the workable. A plan that everyone understands and supports will beat one that is more elegant but that is only accessible to a few. IT needs to find an able and willing external partner in the business. People subprinciples will require some help from Human Resources. Project and portfolio management will require help from all areas of the business, and Finance will have to help with project estimates, budgeting, and post-project analysis. IT and business partnerships require time and attention from all of the other business divisions and functional areas.

The CIO and the rest of the IT leadership team should confidently present the case for technology-driven improvement to the business. If IT may even appear to outshine the business in some way thanks to the suggested changes, push the business to make comparable improvements. Where necessary, conduct competitor analysis or benchmark World Class IT departments to make the case for improvement. IT must drive change.

One thing I have noticed in working with top-notch CIOs is what each of them have in common: the desire to continue to improve. Rather than resting on their past accomplishments, they want to understand where their departments are lagging, not worrying that uncovering trouble spots might be seen as an indictment of them personally. They recognize that a lack of planning and foresight leads to even bigger failures than that which might be uncovered. As Andy Grove, former chairman and CEO of Intel Corporation, made clear in *Only the Paranoid Survive*, it is critically important that one not rest on one's laurels and read only the good press that is written about oneself. In the preface to his book, Grove writes, "Business success contains the seeds of its own destruction.... I believe that the prime responsibility of a manager is to guard constantly against other people's attacks and to inculcate this guardian attitude in the people under his or her management."[1] Focusing attention on where there is still room for improvement or where performance might be slipping will help the IT department and the company more broadly guard against attacks from the outside.

As I mentioned early on in the book, these five principles are not new. Most of the subprinciples are not either. The nuance to the concept of World Class IT is thinking about how performance in one area builds upon the performance in other areas. Of course, this is not to say that the processes are linear. The principles and subprinciples typically operate at the same time. Within each of the five continuums of principle plus subprinciples, improvements in one area can lead to improvements in other areas. Thus each subgrouping operates as a virtuous cycle, just as the five principles do. The opposite is also true, however: neglecting a principle or subprinciple can adversely affect other elements along the same continuum.

I have collaborated with many CIOs who were in the enviable position of adding tremendous value to their business. They were high scorers in principle 4, IT and business partnerships. The CEOs of these companies thought highly of the IT department and its ability to drive positive change for the company. With their focus on business alignment, however, some of these same CIOs ended up neglecting principle 2, infrastructure. As I mentioned in the chapter on infrastructure, this is the most technical of all the principles. If the CIO does not have his or her finger on the pulse of infrastructure, and cannot raise a red flag when new capabilities undertaken in response to the demands of the business create an unsustainable level of complexity, no other division head is going to point that out until something goes terribly wrong. By monitoring all of the principles all the time, these sorts of omissions can likely be avoided. Not only will this sort of across-the-board monitoring make large-scale failures unlikely within the IT department, success in all five principles will enable IT to more easily recruit, train, and retain World Class IT employees.

This journey is not a short one. It can take an IT department several years to see vast improvements among all of the subprinciples. Moreover, it is not realistic to be a high performer in all of the areas covered by the principles and subprinciples. What is important is that all of these areas be monitored and that—thanks to their intimate relationship—corrective action be taken immediately when weaknesses are spotted in any one area.

It is interesting to note that of the five World Class IT principles, only one is truly IT-centric: principle 2, infrastructure. The other four have business implications and can even be borrowed by the business. This is an important distinction, highlighting the fact that the skills the CIO is harnessing are skills that he or she can take to other roles in the company. I believe the universality of the principles is a strength of the World Class IT Methodology. In the book, I have profiled several CIOs who have taken on business responsibilities or become CEOs. As I have mentioned, this is likely to increase, given that so many of the principles and subprinciples can be used in the business. Therefore, the CIO who can guide his or her department to excellent performance in each of these areas will be able to do so in other areas of the company as well. It is for that reason that today's World Class IT leaders will be tomorrow's successful CEOs.

Notes

Introduction

1. Peter High, "Metis Strategy's Forum on World Class IT," podcast interview with Richard Nolan, March 12, 2009.
2. Peter High, "Metis Strategy's Forum on World Class IT," podcast interview with Bob Willett, August 7, 2009.
3. Kim Nash, "CIO to CEO: 56 Moving Up the Ladder," *Baseline*, February 15, 2007.
4. High, podcast interview with Bob Willett.

Chapter One

1. Peter High, "United IT Revamps Processes, Business Relationships to Help Drive Company Forward," *Information Week*, November 9, 2005.
2. Peter High, "Know Thyself and Thy Acquisition." *CIO Digest*, October 2007.

Chapter Two

1. Peter High, "Metis Strategy's Forum on World Class IT," podcast interview with Gregor Bailar, August 19, 2008.

2. Michelle Conlin, "Smashing the Clock: Inside Best Buy's Radical Reshaping of the Workplace," *Business Week*, December 5, 2006.
3. Eric Lundquist, "The IT Skills You Need to Get Through the Recession of 2009," *Upfront*, November 15, 2008. Available at http://blogs.cioinsight.com/lundquist/.
4. Eric Lundquist, "What Makes a Vendor Valuable to a CIO?," *Upfront*, November 18, 2008. Available at http://blogs. cioinsight.com/lundquist/.
5. *Principles of Organizational Behavior Glossary*, Oxford, U.K.: Oxford University Press, 2005.
6. Peter High, "Metis Strategy's Forum on World Class IT," podcast interview with Phaneesh Murthy, November 10, 2008.
7. Dick Grote, *Forced Ranking: Making Performance Management Work* (Cambridge, MA: Harvard Business School Press, 2005).

Chapter Three

1. Peter High, "Metis Strategy's Forum on World Class IT," podcast interview with Tim Harvey, April 16, 2009.
2. "Information Technology—Security Techniques—Code of Practices for Information Security Management," ISO/IEC 27002, first edition, June 15, 2005.
3. Risk Management Solutions, "Tropical Storm Allison, June 2001."
4. Peter High, "Metis Strategy's Forum on World Class IT," podcast interview with Gregor Bailar, August 19, 2009.
5. Scott Berinato, Kathleen Carr, Daintry Duffy, Michael Goldberg, and Sarah Scalet, "Business Continuity and Disaster Recovery Planning: The Basics," CSO *Security and Risk*, April 30, 2008.
6. Sidney Rutberg, "Disaster Recovery: Dealing with Disasters and Short-Term Displacements," *The Secured Lender*, March 1, 2005.

7. Chip Gliedman, "Thirty-One Best Practices for the Service Desk [Executive Summary]," *Forrester Report*, June 28, 2005.

Chapter Four

1. Timothy Lester, Patrick Houston, Joshua Wright, and Juliana Park, "Amazon Your Industry: Extracting Value from the Value Chain," *strategy+business*, First Quarter 2000.
2. Peter High, "Metis Strategy's Forum on World Class IT," podcast interview with John Boushy, December 3, 2008.
3. The Standish Group, "CHAOS Summary 2009," April 23, 2009, www.standishgroup.com/newsroom/chaos_2009.php.
4. Peter High, "Metis Strategy's Forum on World Class IT," podcast interview with Randy Spratt, December 10, 2008.

Chapter Five

1. *"Information Week* Names Harrah's Entertainment's CIO Tim Stanley 'Chief of the Year'," Thomson Reuters, January 23, 2008.
2. Mary Hayes Weier, "Harrah's Innovation Plan: More Pilots, Less PowerPoint," *Information Week*, November 8, 2008.
3. Motorola University. "About Motorola University: The Inventors of Six Sigma," http://www.motorola.com/content.jsp? globalObjectId=3079; accessed May 7, 2009.
4. Brian Hindo, "At 3M, A Struggle Between Efficiency and Creativity," *Business Week*, June 11, 2007.
5. Peter High, "Metis Strategy's Forum on World Class IT," podcast interview with Darko Hrelic, November 10, 2008.
6. Peter High, "Metis Strategy's Forum on World Class IT," podcast interview with Rob Austin, November 10, 2008.
7. Mary J. Benner, and Michael Tushman, "Process Management and Technological Innovation: A Longitudinal Study of the Photography and Paint Industries," *Administrative Science Quarterly*, December 2002.

8. David Greenfield, "How Companies Are Using IT to Spot Innovative Ideas," *Information Week*, November 8, 2008.
9. W. Chan Kim, and Renée Mauborgne, *Blue Ocean Strategy: How to Create Uncontested Market Space and Make the Competition Irrelevant* (Cambridge, MA: Harvard Business School Press, 2005).

Chapter Six

1. Carol Sliwa, "Best Buy to Outsource IT to Accenture," *ComputerWorld*, April 19, 2004.
2. Peter High, "Metis Strategy's Forum on World Class IT," podcast interview with Bob Willett, August 7, 2009.
3. High, podcast interview with Bob Willett.
4. Peter High, "Metis Strategy's Forum on World Class IT," podcast interview with Phaneesh Murthy, November 10, 2008.
5. "IT Outsourcing Trends: Outsourcing Statistics for 11 IT Functions," *Computer Economics*, August 2008.
6. High, podcast interview with Phaneesh Murthy.

Conclusion

1. Andrew Grove, *Only the Paranoid Survive*. (New York: Doubleday Business, 1996).

Bibliography

Benner, Mary J., and Michael Tushman. "Process Management and Technological Innovation: A Longitudinal Study of the Photography and Paint Industries." *Administrative Science Quarterly*, December 2002.

Berinato, Scott, Kathleen Carr, Daintry Duffy, Michael Goldberg, and Sarah Scalet. "Business Continuity and Disaster Recovery Planning: The Basics." CSO *Security and Risk*, April 30, 2008.

Broadbent, Marianne, and Ellen Kitzis. *The New CIO Leader: Setting the Agenda and Delivering Results*. Cambridge, MA: Harvard Business School Press, 2004.

Conlin, Michelle. "Smashing the Clock: Inside Best Buy's Radical Reshaping of the Workplace." *Business Week*, December 5, 2006.

Gliedman, Chip. "Thirty-One Best Practices for the Service Desk [Executive Summary]." *Forrester Report*, June 28, 2005.

Greenfield, David. "How Companies Are Using IT to Spot Innovative Ideas." *Information Week*, November 8, 2008.

Grote, Dick. *Forced Ranking: Making Performance Management Work*. Cambridge, MA: Harvard Business School Press, 2005.

Grove, Andrew. *Only the Paranoid Survive*. New York: Doubleday Business, 1996.

High, Peter. "United IT Revamps Processes, Business Relationships to Help Drive Company Forward." *Information Week*, November 9, 2005.

High, Peter. "Know Thyself and Thy Acquisition." *CIO Digest*, October 2007.

High, Peter. "Metis Strategy's Forum on World Class IT," podcast interview with Gregor Bailar, August 19, 2008.

High, Peter. "Metis Strategy's Forum on World Class IT," podcast interview with Darko Hrelic, November 10, 2008.

High, Peter. "Metis Strategy's Forum on World Class IT," podcast interview with Rob Austin, November 10, 2008.

High, Peter. "Metis Strategy's Forum on World Class IT," podcast tnterview with Phaneesh Murthy, November 10, 2008.

High, Peter. "Metis Strategy's Forum on World Class IT," podcast interview with John Boushy, December 3, 2008.

High, Peter. "Metis Strategy's Forum on World Class IT," podcast interview with Randy Spratt, December 10, 2008.

High, Peter. "Metis Strategy's Forum on World Class IT," podcast interview with Richard Nolan, March 12, 2009.

High, Peter. "Metis Strategy's Forum on World Class IT," podcast interview with Tim Harvey, April 16, 2009.

High, Peter. "Metis Strategy's Forum on World Class IT," podcast interview with Bob Willett, August 7, 2009.

Hindo, Brian. "At 3M, A Struggle Between Efficiency and Creativity." *Business Week*, June 11, 2007.

"Information Technology—Security Techniques—Code of Practices for Information Security Management." ISO/IEC 27002, first edition, June 15, 2005.

"*Information Week* Names Harrah's Entertainment's CIO Tim Stanley 'Chief of the Year'." Thomson Reuters, January 23, 2008.

"IT Outsourcing Trends: Outsourcing Statistics for 11 IT Functions." *Computer Economics*, August 2008.

Kim, W. Chan, and Renée Mauborgne. *Blue Ocean Strategy: How to Create Uncontested Market Space and Make the Competition Irrelevant.* Cambridge, MA: Harvard Business School Press, 2005.

Lester, Timothy, Patrick Houston, Joshua Wright, and Juliana Park. "Amazon Your Industry: Extracting Value from the Value Chain." *strategy+business*, First Quarter 2000.

Lutchen, Mark. *Managing IT as a Business: A Survival Guide for CEOs.* New York: John Wiley & sons, 2003.

Motorola University. "About Motorola University: The Inventors of Six Sigma." http://www.motorola.com/content.jsp?globalObjectId=3079; accessed May 7, 2009.

Nash, Kim. "CIO to CEO: 56 Moving Up the Ladder." *Baseline*, February 15, 2007.

Principles of Organizational Behavior Glossary, Oxford University Press, 2005.

Risk Management Solutions. "Tropical Storm Allison, June 2001."

Ross, Jeanne, Peter Weill, and David Robertson. *Enterprise Architecture As Strategy: Creating a Foundation for Business Execution.* Cambridge, MA: Harvard Business School Press, 2006.

Rutberg, Sidney. "Disaster Recovery: Dealing with Disasters and Short-Term Displacements." *The Secured Lender*, March 1, 2005.

Sliwa, Carol. "Best Buy to Outsource IT to Accenture." *ComputerWorld*, April 19, 2004.

The Standish Group. "CHAOS Summary 2009." www.standishgroup.com /newsroom/chaos_2009.php, April 23, 2009.

Weier, Mary Hayes. "Harrah's Innovation Plan: More Pilots, Less PowerPoint." *Information Week*, November 8, 2008.

Weill, Peter, and Jeanne Ross. *IT Governance: How Top Performers Manage IT Decision Rights for Superior Results*. Cambridge, MA: Harvard Business School Press, 2004.

Index

Page references followed by *fig* indicate an illustrated figure; followed by *t* indicate a table.

A

Accenture, 122
Alignment. *See* Partnership
Allison (Tropical Storm), 49
Amazon.com, 60
"Amazoned" fear, 60
American Express, 23
Ameristar, 101
"Annual Report to GE Share Owners" (General Electric), 28
Austin, Rob, 110

B

Bailar, Gregor, 15–16, 46, 50
Barnes & Noble, 60
Baylor College of Medicine, 49
Benner, Mary, 110
Best Buy: effective outsourcing by, 122–123; ROWE program of, 16–17, 28
Blue Cross and Blue Shield of Kentucky, 101
Blue Ocean Strategy: How to Create Uncontested Market Space and Make the Competition Irrelevant (Kim and Mauborgne), 112–113
Boushy, John, 3, 61, 107
Brenner, Mary, 110
Budgets: external partnering, 139; including placeholder amounts for projects in, 79–80; metrics for, 92t; prioritizing the, 79

Business alignment. *See* Partnership
Business analysis: caution against outsourcing, 128; external partner role in, 140
Business continuity plans: examples of need for, 50–51; external partners for outsourcing role in, 126–127, 139; importance of developing, 49–50; metrics for, 57t; process and steps for developing, 51–53
Business skills, 19
Business strategy: aligning IT with company, 105–106, 116t–117t; creating IT strategy that aligns with, 111–113; external partnering alignment with, 140; prioritizing IT strategic fit of, 70

C

Capital One, 15–16, 46, 50
Career-planning: establishing procedures for, 24–25; metrics for, 30t
CEOs (chief executive officers): dashboards with metrics used by, 3; World Class IT leaders as tomorrow's, 146